KENT HEADLINES

ALAN BIGNELL

KENT HEADLINES

ALAN BIGNELL

COUNTRYSIDE BOOKS
NEWBURY, BERKSHIRE

COUNTRYSIDE BOOKS
3 Catherine Road
Newbury, Berkshire
ISBN 1 85306 059 3

Cover illustration by kind permission of Kent County Library

Typeset by Acorn Bookwork, Salisbury, Wiltshire
Produced through MRM Associates, Reading
Printed in England by J W Arrowsmith Ltd., Bristol

Contents

Introduction

There is no better source of information about the past than local newspapers, where events are reported by local people who live and work among the people and the places that provide the stories. It's a pity – don't you agree? – that we had to wait as long as we did for newspapers. Imagine what it would be like to be able to turn the brittle, discolouring pages of old newspapers, breathing in that distinctive aroma of old newsprint, and to read in, say, the Christmas AD 597 edition of the *Kent Messenger*: 'Tide Turns for Christians: Ten Thousand Baptised in Swale'. Or to leaf through the Restoration Supplement published in May 1660 and read: 'Welcome to Dover, Your Majesty. England Merrie Once More!' What might not the headline writers have made of reports from Faversham in December 1688 that King James II had been caught by Sheppey fishermen in the act of fleeing the country and taken to a local inn to await his return under escort to London? Certainly no modern tabloid journalist could have resisted the temptation: 'HM Held in Queen's Arms!'

Many of the stories that originated in Kent were of much more than local significance. Kent has always been a county where national and even international events have tended to have more impact than they have had in many other parts of the country. Geography has seen to that. For centuries, practically everything of consequence that happened in England involved Kent in some way or another.

News from abroad usually reached the county first simply because it was carried by messengers who brought it through Kent on its way to London. If a monarch travelled abroad, he almost always did so from one of the Kent ports, whether it was Edward II sailing from Dover to his wedding with Isabel the Fair of France in 1308 or Henry VIII bringing perhaps the greatest spectacle ever seen in Kent on its way to the Field of the Cloth of Gold in 1520.

Would-be invaders of England, from Caesar to Hitler, almost invariably aimed their assaults at the Kent coast and it has been Kent that has welcomed emissaries to England, that has helped fugitives to slip quietly away from the country and which has feted famous people who have brought their fame to England with them. It is still so today and is likely to remain so after the Channel Tunnel opens a new Kentish portal into the UK.

This book recalls just a few of the stories that have put Kent into the headlines in the last century or so. Most of them are from the archives of local newspapers and tell of events as they were reported at the time.

Those stories are the flesh and blood of history and I like to think that, during almost thirty years as a newspaper reporter in Kent, I have made my own modest contribution to the history of the county by recording events as I have seen them during that time.

Very early in my career, I was taken to task by an eminent local historian for a minor inaccuracy in one of my stories.

'Journalists,' he lectured me sternly, 'have an awesome responsibility, not just to their readers today but to all future readers who will turn back to their reports expecting to find out exactly what happened.

'If you get it wrong, even in some apparently minor detail, you have falsified history and what actually happened may very well be buried for ever under your imperfect account of what happened.'

Put like that, of course, it's enough to daunt the most self-assured. But I have never forgotten those words and I have always tried to keep them in the forefront of my mind, both when I have been reporting events taking place and also when I have been researching the accounts of other reporters of events before my time. We can all make mistakes, and it is as well to remember it is never wise to rely wholly on any one report of events, but always to check it against others, whenever possible.

In preparing this book, my greatest difficulty was not to find enough suitable stories, but to decide which of the great wealth of stories most deserved to be included.

I have tried to achieve a reasonable mix of local, national and international stories: a fire in which a whole local family was wiped out; the tragic loss of life in a river Thames pleasure steamer accident; the first successful flight by aeroplane across the English Channel.

I have tried, too, to achieve a reasonable emotional mix and to show that headlines do not always have to reflect doom and disaster but may have something to say of achievement and celebration, as well.

But, more than anything else, I have tried to select the sort of stories that readers have always looked for in their favourite newspapers.

I hope you will think I have succeeded.

Alan Bignell
Barming 1989

The Hartlake Hoppers

★

All through the 19th century, a feature of the countryside in Kent was the huge number of casual workers who came, many of them from the very poorest parts of London, to pick hops every year.

Kent was the largest hop-growing county in England and the huge acreage of hops had to be harvested during three or four weeks, usually in September and October. It meant that even a small farm might need several hundred pickers, more than the local population could supply and so the farmers evolved a system of hiring 'strangers' (as they were invariably called by the locals) to live in encampments on their farms during the short but intensive 'hopping' season.

The annual 'hopping down in Kent' was at its height throughout the second half of the century, especially after the railways began to offer cheap fares for the thousands of Londoners who crammed into special trains from London Bridge to places like Paddock Wood and Tonbridge.

Travelling through the pre-dawn hours, they would arrive at their destinations in Kent while the local people were still at breakfast. There they would congregate noisily outside the local railway stations or on village greens to wait for transportation to the various farms, to begin their annual paid 'holiday' in the Garden of England.

On the farms, they lived in camps, sometimes in conditions of considerable squalor, crowded into barns and cart sheds with hard-packed dirt floors covered with straw, or in old Army tents, usually acquired cheaply because they were no longer sufficiently weatherproof for soldiers to live in.

Thousands of Londoners came to Kent for the annual hop-picking season throughout the 19th and early 20th centuries.

As time went by, conditions did improve and most farmers eventually built blocks of 'hopper huts' for their regulars. Even so, well into the 20th century conditions for the hop-pickers continued to be pretty primitive. Yet many of them came back year after year sometimes virtually all their lives and looked forward to the annual hopping as a holiday they would not have missed for anything.

Every hopping season brought its incidents: some funny, some sad. The Londoners, especially the younger ones, were plunged into a totally alien environment where their city-bred instincts exposed them to all sorts of unfamiliar hazards from camp fire burns and scalds to falls out of trees and into ponds and various degrees of poisoning from eating hedgerow fruits and berries.

All these, of course, in addition to the normal domestic hazards made all the more dangerous by the communal living conditions of the hoppers' camps.

10

Some years were marked with outbreaks of illness such as scarlet fever and measles; sometimes even more serious epidemics of typhus and cholera.

Happily, though, although the total accident rate among the hoppers every year throughout the county was high, it was exceptional for a large number of fatalities to occur on any one farm, such as happened on the Cox's farm at Hadlow in October 1853.

It had been an exceptionally wet season that year and the river Medway at Hadlow had overflowed its banks, flooding land on either side.

Farmer Cox's pickers were working in a hop garden on the Hadlow side of the river, although their camp was in the adjoining parish, on the Tudeley side.

On Thursday, 25th October, picking ended for the day and waggoner John Waghorn began the daily chore of ferrying pickers back to their homes on the other side of the river. Naturally, he took the 'home pickers' first – local people, including families of men employed on the farm and also of village tradespeople and others who all welcomed the hop-picking to provide them with the extra money that would buy clothes and other comforts to see them through the coming winter.

When the local people had been safely carried across the river and left to disperse to their own homes, the waggoner drove back to the hop garden to collect about forty of the 'strangers' – Londoners and travellers – whose seasonal home was in the camp on the Tudeley side of the Medway.

It was about 6 pm – the end of a long working day. The pickers had been at their bins since dawn and the waggoner had been collecting up the ten-bushel sacks ('pokes') of hops and taking them to the oast house to be dried all through the day.

The waggon was just about as full as it could be, with people sitting on the sides and the back and crowding

11

together inside to support each other as the heavy waggon (fully loaded as it was it would have weighed about two tons) jolted along in the gathering dusk, drawn by two horses, one in front of the other.

One young hopper had been allowed to ride on the back of the hindmost horse, between the waggon shafts, no doubt to the envy of some of the others in the waggon.

When they reached the Hartlake bridge over the river, Waghorn climbed up on to the back of the lead horse so as not to have to wade through the flood water which spread across the ground at both ends of the timber bridge. It was a

This picture of the bridge, painted after the accident and showing part of the close-boarded side broken away, is owned by Miss R. Hewett.

12

sensible thing to do because the water was up to the horses' knees and quite apart from not wanting to get wet the waggoner would not have been able to control the horses properly in those conditions if he had tried to lead them through the water.

The wooden bridge, which actually belonged to the Medway Navigation Company, had a three-feet close-board fence on each side and metal rungs on the decking which were intended to help horses keep their footing as they climbed up the sharp gradient of the crescent-shaped bridge.

As the lead horse went over the crest of the bridge and was nearing the other side, the horse behind it stumbled. Both riders fought to steady the horses, but the waggon wheel swerved against the boarded side of the bridge with enough weight to break it. Before anything could be done to prevent it, the waggon, with everyone inside it, as well as the two horses and their riders, were thrown into the river.

Because of the heavy rains, the current was running exceptionally fast and, in that moment of tragedy, 30 lives were lost.

The screams and cries for help as the victims were swept downstream in the muddy water were heard at the Bell Inn a mile away in the hamlet of Golden Green. Some of the people who had been sitting on the back and sides of the waggon were able to jump off, on to the bridge, before the waggon fell into the water. They were the lucky ones.

Almost without exception, the rest were drowned, despite the efforts of people who hurried to the spot, attracted by the cries, with lanterns and hop poles and tried to help the people in the water to climb out.

A few were saved in this way, but when the toll was counted, there were only eleven survivors altogether. Of the 30 who drowned, 16 were members of the Leatherland family from the Rosemary Lane area of London. Several of the others were Irish.

13

At the inquest, it was said that the bridge had been in a poor condition for eight or ten years but no-one had thought to tell the owners about it.

The jury returned a verdict of accidental drowning but added that it was entirely because of the defective state of the bridge, which they recommended should be replaced by a substantial construction of either brick or stone.

It was several days before all the victims were recovered. They were buried in one grave in Hadlow churchyard in a series of burials.

The Rev R Shindler, who was one of the first to take an interest in the welfare of hop-pickers in Kent and whose writings about them helped to bring about the later reforms that improved conditions for them considerably, recorded the tragedy and found in it a moral for his readers, too.

He wrote: 'There is something mysterious about the incident, for those 30 persons were all gipsies or Irish and not only had a party of home-dwellers been conveyed across the bridge in safety a short time before, but certain trivial circumstances had prevented several residents uniting with the party that met with so melancholy an end.

'Some may say: "This fact explains all; they were notorious sinners, I doubt not, and God has punished them for their sins with a dreadful sudden death."'

But the parson added his own comment that, in fact, the doomed party may have been no worse than some of the home-dwellers – a somewhat grudgingly charitable thought that has much to say about the way in which the 'strangers', for all they were indispensable to the farmers, were regarded by the local people.

Nevertheless, the Hadlow villagers decided that the victims should not lie unremembered in their communal grave in St Mary's churchyard.

In December that year they decided that a suitable memorial should be erected. It is still there, in a corner of the

14

The Hoppers' Memorial in Hadlow churchyard. The base is engraved with the names of the victims.

churchyard: a monument in the shape of a small pyramid with a cubic base. Until the Second World War claimed them in 1940 for what seemed at the time a more worthy purpose, the stone was enclosed in iron railings. Perhaps some elements of those railings played their part in the Battle of Britain which raged over this part of Kent during another hopping season, almost a century later.

The stone base of the monument is inscribed: 'This monument was erected by public subscription in memory of Thirty Hop Pickers who were drowned at Hartlake Bridge in a Flood of the River Medway on 20th of October, 1853 and whose bodies are buried in this churchyard. In the midst of life we are in death.'

On the other three sides of the base are engraved the names of the drowned hop-pickers.

The inscription and the names are difficult to read now. But the 30 victims of Kent's worst hop-picking tragedy are not forgotten. A small modern metal plate identifies the pyramid as The Hoppers' Memorial and directs attention to a framed account of the incident which hangs just inside the church porch. It is illustrated with pictures of the Hartlake Bridge and the memorial, which flank a hop-wreathed roll of names of those who were drowned.

The World's First Passenger Railway

★

May 3rd, 1830 was a gala day in Canterbury. Cathedral bells rang, guns were fired and the city was decked with flags. At the centre of it all was the station from which the inaugural train on the Canterbury–Whitstable line was to leave on the world's first fully steam-hauled passenger railway journey.

The Canterbury and Whitstable Railway Company had been incorporated in 1825 after years of uncertainty about whether the line would ever be laid.

Canterbury badly needed an alternative means of transporting goods, especially coal, into the city other than along the turnpike road, which was expensive. The city had reached a low point economically after the final collapse of its only manufacturing industry, the weaving of silk and cotton.

Before the 19th century, the only possible alternative to road transport was water, along the river Stour which passes through Canterbury. Over the centuries there had been several proposals for improving the river between Sandwich, where the Stour reached the sea, and Canterbury, but they had all come to nothing, largely because of the distance involved.

Until well into the 18th century, Canterbury's port had been Fordwich, which stood at the highest point of navigation on the river Stour. Caen stone for the building of the cathedral had been unshipped at Fordwich and the same method of transporting goods of all kinds to Canterbury continued for centuries after that.

But it became more and more difficult as silting above Sandwich progressively limited the size of vessels able to reach Fordwich. Every time anyone proposed a waterway, whether it was a river Stour improvement or a purpose-dug canal, the idea floundered on the objection that it was a very long route, especially considering that Canterbury was only some six miles from the nearest coast, at Whitstable.

It was not until George Stephenson demonstrated the practical possibilities of harnessing steam to overland transport that an alternative to the Canterbury–Whitstable turnpike road could be foreseen.

Of course, there remained the problem of Tyler Hill, which reared a formidable barrier between the two towns. If that could be overcome, though, it might be possible to build a railway between them which would be more direct and slightly shorter than the existing turnpike road.

Quite early in the 19th century, solicitor, engineer and coalmaster – and very enthusiastic supporter of railways – William James came to Canterbury to see what were the prospects for a railway there. In 1823 he proposed to the city fathers a line for a railway which, although it was not taken up at the time, was later shortened, made more direct, and adopted for the purposes of promoting an Act of Parliament in order to start work.

A company was formed with £25,000 capital, raised in 500 £50 shares, which James estimated would be enough to cover the costs of building the railway. He was wrong. He may have been a good solicitor and coalmaster; even a good engineer. But he was not reliable when it came to finance, his own included.

By the time the Act of Parliament received Royal Assent in June 1825, James had been declared bankrupt and imprisoned for debt and he therefore fell out of the picture at

Canterbury. The company turned to George Stephenson for advice.

Stephenson was already renowned for his locomotives and his famous *Rocket* had become something of a modern wonder by achieving the incredible speed of almost 30 mph.

He advised the Canterbury company to increase its capital and in return the company appointed him its Engineer, although he personally only visited Canterbury once or twice. The actual on-site work was done by assistants of his, including his son Robert.

Tunnelling through Tyler Hill began on the last day of October 1825 and it was the Channel tunnel of its day in Kent, attracting crowds of people on outings to see the work in progress.

It was estimated that almost two and a half million bricks would be needed to line the tunnel. The tunnellers worked by night to dig out six feet of tunnel so that bricklayers could follow behind them, bricking it in, by day.

The railway was finally completed in 1830, after more than four years of work. A number of financial problems had to be overcome during that time, but at last it was done.

The day of the opening of the new railway was a grand occasion indeed, and crowds gathered in fields on both sides of the track to witness the spectacle of passengers being hauled along by steam.

Passengers had travelled by rail before, but only in carriages drawn by horses, operating in the same way that canal boats were pulled along a towpath. This time, for the first time in the world, passengers – real people! – were to experience travel at the mercy of engines powered by steam.

The train was assembled at the Canterbury end of the line. In the first carriage were the directors of the railway company, all wearing white rosettes. In the second carriage were the aldermen and other members of Canterbury Corporation and in the third, their ladies.

Crowds gathered to see the spectacle when the world's first steam-hauled passenger railway train left Canterbury for Whitstable in May 1830.
(Picture: Copyright Canterbury Heritage Museum)

The fourth truck contained the band which was to provide music along the way and carriages five to ten were occupied by proprietors of the railway and their many friends.

Journalists who witnessed the scene described it as 'the gayest of the gay'. The day was remarkably fine and great crowds had gathered to see the procession start at 11 am. When the trucks began to move, pulled by a rope wound by the stationary engine at the first of the two engine stations, there was a loud cheer and guns were fired.

The *Maidstone Journal and Kentish Advertiser* reported: 'The fields on each side of the line of the road, being crowded by well-dressed people of all ages, presented one of the most lively scenes we have witnessed for some time.'

Altogether, there were 20 carriages and twelve wagons to

make that first journey from Canterbury to Whitstable by rail, with nearly 300 people on board.

The most thrilling moments of the whole journey for them were the three and a quarter minutes it took to go through the 828 yard-long tunnel, in pitch darkness. But one traveller afterwards described the journey as an altogether delightful one, taking 41½ minutes, in motion, from start to finish.

The first of the two 25 hp high pressure steam engines was housed at the top of Tyler Hill and the train was hauled from Canterbury North Lane station to there by means of a rope and winding drum.

At the Tyler Hill engine house, the rope was unhooked and another rope was attached to haul the train by another stationary engine to the next station, at Clowes Wood. From there, the line went downhill and passenger carriages were

The steam locomotive Invicta *pushed the trucks with their VIP passengers the last two miles to Whitstable.*
(Picture: Copyright Canterbury Heritage Museum)

21

detached from the goods wagons and allowed to freewheel at speeds of up to 30 mph. At the bottom, the carriages were checked by a brake on the wheels. The goods wagons were also allowed to run down, but with a rope attached to control their speed.

Four miles of the total journey thus covered, at a point known as Bogshole, the 10 hp locomotive *Invicta*, modelled on the original *Rocket*, was coupled to the carriages and wagons and, driven by Edward Fletcher, who had brought it to Canterbury from Newcastle, it hauled the train the remaining two miles into Whitstable at about 12 mph.

Again the *Maidstone Journal and Kentish Advertiser*: 'At first starting, the quiet power with which the vast mass was set in motion dispelled every fear in the passengers. The entrance into the tunnel was very impressive – the total darkness – the accelerated speed – the rumbling of the cars – the loud cheering of the whole party echoing through the vault, combined to form a situation almost terrific – certainly novel and striking.'

The celebrations of the day were crowned at 7 pm with a dinner for about 150 people at the King's Head Hotel, Canterbury. One of the guests was Robert Stephenson, son of the supervising engineer, who made a speech of which attending journalists could only report: 'He spoke so low that the representatives of the Press could not hear distinctly what he said.'

The railway opened for business the next day, 4th May. Carriage by train cost only about half as much as by road carrier. There was a comprehensive bill of charges for different commodities, which included bedsteads 9d, salt water 3s 6d ton, and bags of feathers 6d cwt. Passengers were charged 9d, or 6d for children under twelve years old.

There was an hourly service at first, ten trains each way with the first one leaving Canterbury at 9 am daily except Sunday.

In 1832 a Sunday service was begun. It was a bit more expensive than the weekend one because, being 'passenger only', fares were not subsidised by freight charges, but it was very popular with trippers from Canterbury and the surrounding countryside, who headed for a half-day by the sea. The trains only ran the Sunday service in the afternoon in order not to interfere with morning church services but even so it drew protests and was withdrawn after a petition against it was presented to the company by the local clergy.

Up to this time, Whitstable had been a fairly insignificant little seaside town, noted for its Native oysters but nothing else. The new harbour was expected to give Canterbury its link with London (its 'facility for communication with the great Metropolis' as the journals of the day put it) and by enabling salt water to be conveyed to Canterbury, make it possible for the city to have its own baths.

It was two years after the railway opened that Whitstable harbour was finally completed and ready for business. It opened on 19th March, 1832. But by 1841 the railway company had run into financial difficulties and both the railway and the harbour were advertised To Let at an annual rent of not less than £3,500 for a seven-year lease. It was not exactly the bargain of the year, and one offer of £3,000 was refused.

When the line was surveyed in 1843, it was found to be in a badly dilapidated state and had to be completely overhauled. *Invicta* did not work well and was taken out of service much sooner than might have been expected, although it has survived a long period of exposure to public curiosity on an open-air site near the city centre and is today preserved in greater care in the Stour Street heritage centre in the old Poor Priests' Hospital.

Eventually, the South Eastern Railway took over the lease and operated the line from Michaelmas 1844. In 1846, the company rebuilt the line for locomotive use only.

Until that time, no locomotive had hauled trains through

Invicta *locomotive now in the Canterbury Heritage Museum.*
(Picture: Copyright Canterbury City Museums)

the Tyler Hill Tunnel, so there was no smoke in it. Once the locomotives began to use it, however, there began to be complaints from passengers, especially those travelling in the open third-class carriages, that they felt as though they were being suffocated when they went through the tunnel.

Nevertheless, from then passenger trains covered the distance in about 20 minutes, with no stops. Before that, running time had increased until it was taking up to an hour.

In 1853 the lessors agreed to sell the railway outright to the South Eastern, which continued to operate it for both freight and passengers until 1st January 1931, when the passenger service was ended.

The line was closed completely on 1st December 1952 (although it was reopened temporarily after the disastrous east coast flooding in 1953) and soon afterwards the line was dismantled, although the route was preserved for a time as a public path.

The famous 'slewed' bridge over Church Road (now Old Bridge Road) at Tankerton was built to carry the line in 1826–30 and was the oldest railway bridge in the world when it was demolished for road widening in 1969, sweeping away the last remaining feature of the line which became known, because of its Canterbury and Whitstable initials and its seaside character, as the dear old Crab and Winkle line.

The Big Freeze

★

It is not true that all newspapers have headline type already set up and held in readiness from one year to another for the unfailing reliability of the newsworthiness of the English weather.

They could do. Few years pass without the inevitable 'Snow Chaos', or 'It's a Scorcher!' headlines bearing down heavily on the smaller type reports of exceptionally heavy snowfalls or unusually prolonged heatwaves.

Floods, drought, gales – the headline writers love them, although the stories below do not always justify their exuberance.

The great frost that held Kent in its grip for six deadly weeks in 1895 came at a time when headlines were rather more restrained, at least in size, but they could not diminish the bitterness of that winter.

Maidstone's oldest inhabitant – unnamed – was tracked down to confess that he could not recall a frost lasting so long with such intensity.

It was certainly more than 40 years since the mouth of the river Medway froze over from Sheerness Dockyard to the Isle of Grain so that only steamers could force a way through and they only at great risk to their paddles. Men who went ashore from HMS *Thunderer* one Friday night were unable to return on Saturday morning and on Saturday afternoon a boat for Sheerness Dockyard from HMS *Landrail* became embedded in an ice floe and was carried round Garrison Point towards the sea.

The 1895 freeze made possible a journey across the ice in The Swale, between mainland Kent and the Isle of Sheppey.

It was actually towed back to safety, still embedded in the ice, by the Sheerness government tug with the harbour-master himself on board.

Around the Sheppey coast, ice piled up for eight or nine miles, reaching a mile out to sea, and passenger steamers plying between Sheerness and Port Victoria on the Isle of Grain had to smash their way through the ice, taking more than an hour on what was normally a ten minute trip to connect up with South Eastern Railway trains for London.

At Chatham Naval Dockyard, 25° of frost was recorded and the dock basins were iced 'to a great depth'. Above Rochester bridge, the river Medway was frozen solid, from bank to bank. Snow swept up from the city streets and tipped into the river to get rid of it, froze into great bergs of granite-hard ice where it landed.

The whole 17 miles of the river Medway between Maid-stone and Tonbridge was frozen, bringing all barge traffic to a halt. Many vessels had to turn back or anchor at sea because they were unable to enter the river Thames at Gravesend because of the barrier of ice floes there.

The Woolwich free ferry, which normally took almost a thousand workmen to and from work every day, had to stop running, seriously affecting work in factories on both sides of the river.

In fact, things became so bad along the Thames, that a thousand men who made their living on the river in one way or another applied to magistrates for advice about where they could turn for assistance, claiming that they and their families were starving because they could not work.

Things were no better at the other end of the county. The Dover dock froze over and ice stretched 200 yards out to sea at Whitstable. It caused hardship for the town's fishermen, but brought hundreds of sightseers into the town.

Many people literally froze to death, including several cabmen and omnibus drivers. East London Coroner Mr Wynne Baxter spent the whole of one day holding inquests on victims of cold and want resulting from inability to work because of the weather. He dealt with no fewer than 30 cases in two days and was reported as saying that he was having to contemplate holding inquests on Sundays as well if the freeze did not relent.

The mail man from Staplehurst to Chatham floundered through snow drifts and into a field where he finally had to abandon the mail cart and complete the journey on the back of the horse, arriving hours late and completely exhausted.

There was no unemployment dole at that time, of course, and most of the thousands of men who were thrown out of work had to rely solely upon charity to keep them and their families from starving. Relief committees were set up in all the towns and at a special meeting in Chatham the Mayor led donations to a distress fund with a cheque for two guineas, which he later increased to five guineas after Lord Charles Beresford sent a donation of ten pounds.

In Maidstone, the soup kitchen's water main froze and there was no soup for the thousand hungry applicants. Instead, they had to make do with bread. Once the water was restored, the kitchen was serving a thousand quarts of soup a day to nearly 25,000 people.

The town also reopened a stone quarry specially to provide relief work for between 20 and 30 men and another hundred men were set to work clearing snow from the town's streets.

At nearby Sutton Valence, a public meeting in the National School Room raised more than £20 for food relief and it was decided that each individual needing help should receive one loaf of bread and some cheese while the hard weather

Ships and barges became ice-bound, some for two weeks, and some sank under the weight of the ice around them.

29

The ice in The Swale threatened to crush Medway barges that became frozen into it.

continued. In fact, it was afterwards reported, 44 families were relieved on one Saturday alone with 138 loaves and 22 pounds of cheese.

The report noted: 'The poor creatures were exceedingly thankful.'

Many towns and villages were without water when supplies froze solid and the residents had to rely entirely upon water carts, which were more usually employed in the summer to go along the streets laying the dust.

Worse even than that, though, for some people at least, was the calamitous freezing up of beer engines in some of the public houses! Some landlords could not even draw beer from the barrels in their cellars because the beer itself was frozen in the spigots.

The ancient ferries across the river Medway just down-stream of Maidstone at Newhythe, Snodland and Halling could not continue to operate because of the ice – something that had not happened more than a very few times since those same ferries were used by Chaucerian pilgrims travelling to Canterbury. Unfortunately, the ice was not reliably thick enough for the foiled passengers to walk across and they had to walk many miles to cross the river by way of the equally ancient stone bridge at Aylesford in order to get to work, adding hours to their long working days.

But – it's an ill wind that blows nobody any good and every cloud has a silver lining.

The great lake at Mote Park in Maidstone was the scene of the greatest ice carnival in living memory and there were similar fetes on lakes and ponds all over the county.

The Mote Park lake was illuminated after dark with burning tar barrels and huge bonfires, both on the ice itself and on the banks. Chinese lanterns and coloured lights transformed the scene into a spectacular wonderland and many of the skaters carried flares and torches as they skimmed about on the ice to the accompaniment of music played for them by the band of the Queen's Own Royal West Kent Regiment.

One newspaper reporter described the scene – with some justification, one can imagine – as 'the most beautiful imaginable.'

Altogether, some 5,000 people paid more than £116 to skate on the frozen lake.

At nearby Linton Park, home of Lord Cornwallis, the lake was also the venue for an ice carnival. Here, too, the ice was illuminated with lanterns and fairy lights and little lamps were set into miniature grottoes created in the snow round the edge of the lake. With the skaters carrying flares of different colours and a grand fireworks display ending with the singing of the National Anthem by the crowd, no wonder there were resounding cheers for the host, Squire Cornwallis and his wife when the evening finally ended.

At Staplehurst, another village not far from Maidstone, a lake owned by Mr W. Hoare was loaned to two ten-men cricket teams who played on the ice. The visitors, who came from the surrounding countryside, beat the Staplehurst home team by 49 runs to 45, but afterwards, with energy to spare, the two sides changed the game to hockey and then the Staplehurst men took their revenge with a 9-0 defeat of their visitors.

There have been other great frosts since then, but times have changed. If later generations enjoyed their winters with a harsher, more frenzied gaiety, at least they have, for the most part, suffered less hardship during them, as well. Most of us would be prepared to accept it was a fair exchange.

The Great Swim

★

The English Channel still represents perhaps the greatest test of endurance a swimmer can attempt.

The straight line distance from Shakespeare Cliff at Dover to Cap Griz Nez off Calais is about 21 miles. Far enough, but plenty of people have swum farther than that. The special challenge of the Channel lies in the very strong currents, the cold, and such irritants as jellyfish stings capable of paralysing a swimmer temporarily, for good measure.

Even on that mythical fine day when, locals claim, it is possible to see the cliffs of France on the other side, the cross-Channel swimmer must expect to have to swim at least 30 miles and to be in the water for upwards of 20 hours.

It is not a feat to be embarked upon by the faint-hearted, nor by anyone without a great deal of determination and stamina.

Until 1875, no man had ever swum from England to France. Or, rather, there was no official record of anyone having done so. Ever since the Napoleonic wars there had been stories of French prisoners who braved the swim rather than remain aboard the prison hulks moored in the river Medway.

Certainly, some did escape from the hulks. Others were drowned trying to do so. A few of those who reached the banks were helped by local smugglers who ran a lucrative sideline in repatriating French officers (more rarely other ranks, who were unlikely to be able to find the large sums of money demanded for the service!). But stories of desperate men who, unable to buy a passage home from one of the Kent smuggling gangs specialising in the work, found their way to Dover and succeeded in swimming home to France persisted. None, however, was ever verified.

In April 1875, an American life-saver called Capt Paul Boyton demonstrated an American-designed inflatable rubber suit by attempting to float in it across the Channel. It was a publicity stunt and Boyton simply lay on his back in the inflated suit and, using a double bladed paddle, propelled himself out to sea where he fitted a specially designed mast and sail into a socket in his boot! In this way he covered about 50 miles, but even so he did not reach France on that occasion, although he later tried the return trip and succeeded in reaching the South Foreland after nearly 24 hours in the water.

By 1875, Capt Matthew Webb was already a national figure. He was a doctor's son, born in Shropshire in 1848, but he was brought up beside the river Severn where he learned to swim as a young boy.

He became a merchant naval officer and although many of his seagoing friends thought he was a pretty indifferent swimmer because he was not as fast they were in the water, he was very strong and had great endurance. He once dived overboard to rescue a man who fell out of the rigging of a ship into the icy Atlantic during a gale and was in the water more than 35 minutes before he was picked up. He did not save the life of the other man, but he did receive a Royal Humane Society gold medal for the attempt.

The following year he became a ship's captain but by then it was already his intention to become a professional swimmer and the first man to swim across the English Channel.

He had completed several notable swims before July 1875, when he bet £10 at two to one that he could swim down the Thames from Blackwall to Gravesend, a distance of about 20 miles, on the ebb tide. He did it in under five hours, setting a record that stood for 24 years.

Later the same month he swam round the coast from Dover to Ramsgate in eight hours and forty minutes, some of the time against the tide.

So he knew he could swim the distance across the Channel and he was confident he could stay in the water the necessary length of time. He was 27 years old, weighing some 14½ stone stripped for the water; almost six feet tall with a 40 inch chest. Doctors who examined him declared him to be in perfect health.

Despite the evidence of Capt Boyton's crossing that it was

Captain Matthew Webb.

easier to cross from France to England than from England to France – a fact well appreciated by modern Channel swimmers – Webb's first attempt at the cross-Channel swim began in Dover on 12th August, 1875, after a four-day wait for the right conditions. As he stood on Admiralty Pier, all he was waiting for was the tide, but when that turned, the until-then almost perfect weather suddenly worsened.

Throughout his wait, he had had the constant company of a little group of journalists, all waiting to record for eager readers the success or failure of this historic attempt. Some of them – or their editors – were beginning to tire of all the delays and wonder if it was worth the expense of remaining in Dover any longer.

Knowing that, Webb decided that, whatever the weather, he would embark upon his cross-Channel swim and hope for the best.

The English Channel is not noted for its forebearance or for its concern with human aspirations. Its very capriciousness has, again and again through English history, been the salvation of this island nation. It had no more regard then for one brave individual than it had had for a whole armada of Spanish invasion ships.

As Webb waded into the sea, the wind was increasing in strength. They were not far out from the shore before most of the journalists who were crowded into the escorting lugger, were very seasick and fervently wishing the swim had been postponed just once more!

After covering seven miles in five hours, Webb was persuaded to abandon the attempt and to finish the journey to Calais by boat.

Although the attempt had failed, it had fired the public imagination and a group of members of the Stock Exchange offered him sponsorship of 25 guineas each. It was a generous offer and it meant that Webb could afford to try again, which he did, twelve days later, on 24th August.

Captain Matthew Webb accepting brandy from his escort to take away the pain of jellyfish stings during his first successful attempt to swim the Channel.

Greased overall in porpoise oil, he waded into the water at about one o'clock in the afternoon and launched himself for France. This time the sea was in a good mood. It was dead calm and, sustained by beef tea, hot coffee and ale, Webb swam so strongly that the oarsmen in the escorting lugger had to pull with all their strength to keep up with him.

The swimmer was a major attraction. Cross-Channel ferries altered course to give passengers a glimpse of him and a school of porpoises, perhaps lured by the thick covering of oil, came to escort him some of the way. Less welcome were the jellyfish, which stung him so painfully that he broke his own rule and accepted some brandy to try to take away the pain.

When the tide turned, he was still three miles from France and was carried further out and along the French coast where, for the next five hours, he swam frustratingly almost parallel with, and no more than about a mile away from, his goal.

When he finally put his feet down on French soil, he had been in the water for 21 hours and 45 minutes and had covered nearly 40 miles.

But he was, by all the record books, the first man to swim the English Channel.

The French were almost as excited about it as the English were. People who had gathered to welcome him sang *Rule Britannia* as he was helped up the beach to where a horse and trap waited to take him to the local Hotel de Paris.

There, he took a bath and went straight to bed, but not to sleep. The hotel landlord, recognising the publicity value to himself of his celebrated guest, had arranged for the local band to play for him out in the street under his window!

After trying to ignore the noise, Webb finally left his bed, went to the window and told the bandsmen, in the sort of Anglo-Saxon English that left nothing to the French imagination, to go away. They did, and he finally got to sleep.

He awoke to find himself a national hero and an international celebrity. The *Daily Telegraph* declared: 'Capt Webb is at this moment probably the best known and most popular man in the world.'

Two days after wading ashore in France, Webb was back in Dover, quite recovered, he said, and fully ready for all the feting that was to follow.

The Mayor of Dover welcomed him back with the words: 'I don't believe that in the future history of the world any such feat will be performed by anyone else.'

It may not have been the biggest mistake the mayor ever made, but it must have been a close contender. By 1988 the swim had been completed by 359 swimmers of many different nationalities.

Within a week, subscriptions to a Capt Webb testimonial

fund had reached £1,000 and wherever he went police had to be called out to clear a path through crowds of admirers who flocked to congratulate him.

Before the end of the year he had written a book called *The Art of Swimming*, and with his testimonial fund topping £2,500 he began to issue challenges to other swimmers for all sorts of money-raising feats.

In 1880 he married, in London, but he was 35 now and no longer able to perform as a swimmer as he once had. Although he was still a major attraction in England and America, his heyday was over. Some of his engagements made him very little money and he began to be a kind of national sideshow, undertaking more and more desperate stunts just to earn money to keep himself and his family.

In 1883 he chose to attempt to swim across the top of the Niagara Falls. Just about everyone advised him not to do it. His would not be the first attempt. In 20 years, some 80 people had lost their lives in the rapids, but Webb was convinced he had worked out a way of doing it successfully.

In fact, the rapids won the contest. Webb's body was found eight miles downstream at the village of Lewiston, New York.

More than 70 attempts were made in the years following to repeat Capt Webb's historic cross-Channel swim. They all failed. It was not until September 1911 that 37 year old T W Burgess of Rotherham swam from South Foreland to Le Chatelet, a mile east of Cap Griz Nez, in 22 hours and 30 minutes. It was his twelfth attempt.

Crash!

Henry Benge stood with his gang of platelayers and carpenters at the side of the track as the 2.50 pm train crossed the timbered Beult Viaduct near Staplehurst in Kent.

The train puffed over the 70 yards long bridge, known locally as Hockenbury Bridge, trailing its plume of steamy smoke over the carriages and down on to the men at the trackside, who stared up at the driver and fireman on the footplate as the locomotive passed them.

As soon as the train had rumbled on its way, puffing contentedly along the line that ran almost dead straight and level for about 24 miles between Ashford and Tonbridge, Henry Benge marshalled the gang back to their work.

As foreman, it was his job to make sure the line was clear for the work to go ahead. To help him do that, he had a copy of the South Eastern Railway Company's time book. He had no watch, but he did not need one. He took the time from the passing trains. With the 2.50 safely past, his book told him that no other train was due to cross the bridge today, Friday, 9th June, 1865, until the boat train, which was due at 4.15 pm.

'Right, men,' he told them. 'Plenty of time to get those two lengths of rail up and the beam beneath them replaced before the boat train is due.'

The men bent to their work. The bridge had been under repair for three months and Benge was pleased to be working on it because it was only a couple of miles west of Headcorn, where he lived with his wife and three young children. It was an easy walk to work and back home again at the end of the day.

He was 33 years old and had worked for the railway company for ten years. His record was good enough for him to have been entrusted with the supervision of gangs like this one on a number of occasions, and he was paid a guinea a week for the extra responsibility, while others in the gang earned only 18 shillings.

Although he could not read or write particularly well, Henry Benge could interpret the timetable well enough.

Hockenbury Bridge was a construction of iron girders spanned by 25 ft long wooden beams to which the rails were fixed. There was no parapet or rail and 15 feet below the top of the bridge the little river Beult that gave the viaduct its railway company name had about two feet of muddy water flowing over about six feet of soft mud. The seven brick buttresses supporting the bridge seemed almost superfluous now, but in times of heavy rainfall a much greater volume of water rushed under it and flooding was common in this part of the Weald of Kent. Even in June, the land on either side of the river was marshy and soft.

Benge walked a little way along the track towards where he had sent one of the men, John Wiles, with the red flag. There was no need to go all the way to him. Wiles had done the job of flagman often enough and he was clearly in position, the usual ten telegraph poles (about 550 yards) east of the bridge.

The foreman relaxed. All was as it should be.

The work on the bridge involved renewing the 32 timbers and all but one had already been renewed. That remaining one was at the Headcorn end and the gang had to take up two 21 ft lengths of rail in order to remove the beam and replace it with a new one.

The boat train from Folkestone did not run at the same time every day. Its departure time was governed by the

41

'Appalling Accident on the South Eastern Railway' read the headlines in the South Eastern Gazette *on Tuesday, 13th June 1865, over its report of the Staplehurst Rail Crash that involved Charles Dickens.*

arrival of the cross-Channel ferry, which in turn depended upon the tides. The boat train was sometimes known as the tidal train.

Misreading one line on the company time book could, therefore, mean a difference of an hour in the train's expected departure time and, consequently, its arrival at any given point along the route, which was scheduled non-stop to Redhill.

Flagman Wiles saw the approaching train first, while it was still on the far side of Headcorn station, perhaps as much as three miles away from the bridge. By the time he had realised the implication of what he saw and shouted to the men on the bridge to attract their attention over the clamour of their work, the train was no more than about a mile away.

The men on the bridge looked up and saw Wiles waving his flag wildly at the oncoming train.

Benge went white. Dry-mouthed, he gasped: 'God! It's the boat train! What shall we do?'

There was nothing they could do but scramble clear of the ruptured track as quickly as they could.

On the boat train, driver Crombie was looking at the track and he saw Wiles standing in his way, waving his red flag in a frenzy of excitement. Realising there was some kind of danger ahead, the driver tugged on the train whistle, two quick pulls sounding the danger signal of two whistle blasts close together. At the same time, he shut off steam and applied the brakes.

The train had left Folkestone at 2.30 pm. It was the following day, on Saturday, it was due to run some two hours later. It had aboard its 14 carriages, seven of which were first class, about 110 passengers 'chiefly moving in the higher circles of life' as a newspaper report described them subsequently, most of whom were booked through from Paris to London, an eight-hour journey.

It was pulled by one of the most powerful engines belonging to the South Eastern Railway Company and included the tender, luggage van and brake car.

At the time the driver first saw the frantic flagman on the line ahead of him, the train would have been travelling at about 50 mph, and it had covered about 30 miles from Folkestone when it passed through Headcorn at full speed.

The whole train was equipped with five brakes, plus the tender brake, and there were three guards on the train. But despite the braking, the train was still travelling at an estimated 30 mph when it reached the bridge. Its impetus was enough to carry the engine across the 21 ft gap, snapping one of the bridge girders as it did so, and back on to the rails on the other side. It dragged the tender with it, as well as the first brake van and two of the first class carriages.

But eight of the carriages toppled over, off the bridge and into the muddy water below. Two other carriages were left hanging over the side of the bridge at either end of the train, still attached to the coaches immediately behind and in front of them.

The train was completely shattered. Escaping steam hissed and added to the cries of the terrified passengers. It was all over in a moment or two and then, except for the steam and the cries, there was that sudden stillness that follows a catastrophe of that kind.

It was a lonely spot. There were open fields on both sides of the track and the noise of the crash was distinctly heard a very long way off. From fields and cottages and homes as far back along the line as Headcorn people came hurrying to the spot.

Many of the passengers had scrambled out of the train and into the water, where they had become stuck in the deep, soft mud.

Messages were rushed to London Bridge and a special train carried South Eastern general manager Eborell and other company representatives, including two surgeons and other medical men to the scene.

Help was also sent from Ashford, Tonbridge, Staplehurst, Marden and other villages and small towns on either side of the disaster bridge.

By the time all were assembled there were 20 medical men on the scene. Staplehurst surgeon Mr Wilkins converted his home into a hospital and other local residents put their homes at the disposal of the injured. Schoolmistress Miss Lord and others volunteered as nurses.

But despite their efforts, ten passengers lost their lives and 50 people were injured.

Among the passengers on the train was the celebrated author, Charles Dickens. He was returning from a holiday in France with the actress Ellen Ternan and her mother, also an actress.

After the derailment, in which he and his travelling companions were all flung together into a corner of the compartment, they found they were in one of the two undamaged carriages remaining, more or less, on the rails. It was tilted over the edge of the bridge in what Dickens himself described in a letter to a friend as an apparently impossible manner.

He calmed the two ladies as best he could and climbed out of the carriage on to the step, from where he could see people scrambling from other carriages and plunging down into the water or the marshy fields beside it, either believing that they would be safer there or unaware of the height of the drop and the nature of the landing.

Summing up the situation, Dickens went back into the carriage where he urged the ladies to remain still and quiet while he rummaged through his luggage and found a half-bottle of brandy he was bringing home with him. With that strung round his neck, he climbed down the brickwork of the bridge to do what he could for the injured.

Charles Dickens helped other victims of the Staplehurst train crash.

He knew a lot more about writing than he did about first aid and although he may not have been responsible since their condition may have put them beyond help in any case, nevertheless it seems that at least two people to whose lips he put the bottle of brandy died very soon afterwards.

Using his hat as a basin, he scooped up river water to bathe wounds. Some of the people he tried to help in this way also died before more expert help reached them.

His own faith in the restorative powers of brandy, however, seems to have been unshakeable, for he later returned to the carriage and found another whole bottle which he sacrificed to succour the unfortunate victims of the crash.

Afterwards, his work for the injured was recognised by directors of the South Eastern Railway Co, who sent him a letter of appreciation and a gift.

As well as the two ladies, Dickens had with him on the journey his latest episode of *Our Mutual Friend*, which was being published in instalments, ready for the printers.

Although not actually injured in the accident, Dickens did suffer from delayed shock and recurrent nightmares afterwards. He was, after all, 53 years old and for the rest of his life he no longer enjoyed travel of any kind, though he was to do quite a lot of it. Friends found it significant that, after a marked deterioration in his health, he finally died, at his Gad's Hill, Kent, home in 1870 on the anniversary of the train crash, 9th June.

After the passengers were all removed, the gangers were able to get to work clearing the track. It took 150 of them all day Saturday and part of Sunday morning to complete the work.

An inquest was opened at the Railway Hotel, Staplehurst at 4 pm on Saturday, when the Coroner spoke of 'the most lamentable event that has happened on the main line of the South Eastern Railway.' The railway had had a generally very good accident record until then, since the line between Redhill and Ashford was opened in 1842.

The inquest was told company rules required that when rails were taken up, detonating signals should be placed on the track every 250 yards for 1,000 yards, ending with two detonators and a red flag. So there should have been five detonators in place and the flagman should have been 1,000 yards from the bridge, not the 500 or 600 yards Wiles said he was.

The guard on the train estimated the speed of the train when he first applied the brakes at 45–50 mph and although expert evidence judged the train to have hit the bridge at about 30 mph, it was reckoned that the train could have been stopped in time if the proper safety precautions had been taken.

Joseph Gallimore was the district inspector of the permanent way and was responsible for the work of the gang under the foremanship of Henry Benge. Gallimore said he did not ask if detonating signals were being used.

Benge admitted he read the details in his time book for Saturday instead of Friday and both he and Gallimore were charged with manslaughter. The flagman Wiles and train driver Crombie were both exonerated from blame by the Coroner.

Benge and Gallimore came before a special magistrates' court at Cranbrook, where Benge found himself without representation because his solicitor failed to turn up. The hearing went ahead, however, and Benge could only say in his own defence that he was sorry for his mistake.

He told the court he was not much of a scholar but he could just read and write. The company rule book was handed to him and he was required to sign for it without being asked if he had read it or not.

The inspector, Gallimore, told the Bench he was responsible for many different gangs and could not be in 20 different places at once to make sure rules were being obeyed. His defence solicitor argued for him that if he were to be held responsible, then clearly so must others higher up the Company's chain of command.

Both men were committed for trial at assizes and remanded on bail.

There was a Board of Trade inquiry, held in July 1865, which decided the train would probably have reached London in safety, even with the rails up on the viaduct, if the company rules had been followed. The Board decided Gallimore must have known the rules were being disobeyed – and if he didn't, he should have done – and called for a tightening up of rules and measures for preventing similar accidents in future.

At the Kent Summer Assizes that year, Benge and Gallimore both pleaded not guilty to manslaughter.

In evidence, Head Engineer Ashcroft said he had been with the company for eleven years and knew that company rules required a foreman to be provided with a watch, but he said the company had never given watches to foremen during his time.

However, he added, there were in fact seven watches among the nine men employed on the bridge at the time of the accident, even though Benge, the foreman, did not have one of them.

After a short retirement, the jury returned a verdict of guilty against Benge, who was sentenced to nine months' hard labour.

At the direction of the judge, Gallimore was acquitted.

The Snodland Tragedy

★

Murder always makes headlines. The murder of a policeman is, even now, thankfully a sufficiently rare occurrence to be sure of getting a good deal of news coverage.

Until August 1873, no Kent policeman had ever been murdered. When one was, it inevitably created a great deal of public interest and inspired such headlines as 'Frightful Murder at Snodland' and 'The Snodland Tragedy' in the county's principal newspaper, the *South Eastern Gazette*.

The murder happened one Sunday night – or, rather, early Monday morning – and the sequence of events that led up to it was unfolded in a series of stories in the paper, from that of the discovery of the body to the report of the trial and sentencing of the murderer.

The victim was Police Constable (second class) No 190 Israel May, the local bobby who lived in the cement-making Medway village of Snodland. He had been a labourer until, aged 23, he enrolled as a policeman, 14 years previously.

The village was very much smaller then than it is now. It had been an agricultural village for centuries until the building boom of the early 19th century brought the cement industry to this part of Kent beside the river Medway. In the 50 years between 1801 and 1851 the population of the village doubled and by 1881, after the arrival of the Strood–Maidstone railway, it leaped to almost three thousand.

One of the biggest employers in the whole of the Lower Medway Valley was the Snodland Paper Mill of Charles Townsend Hook, and other industries were established

50

there, too. Men looking for work drifted towards this part of Kent from all over the country, seeking employment in the new riverside industries. They earned good money for the time but they had nothing to spend it on but drink, which was available in plenty at pubs like The Bull, to which they resorted especially at weekends.

The only representative of law and order in Snodland was PC May. Inevitably, he found it necessary from time to time to utter warnings and remonstrances to customers of The Bull who caused unacceptable noise or nuisance after they had downed a few drinks. One such man was Thomas Atkins, a labourer who, at one time, worked for the Burham Cement Co.

Burham was a village on the opposite side of the river Medway to Snodland; a village which had, if anything, rather less to offer in the way of an occasional night out than Snodland had.

High Street, Snodland, 1864 – from a painting believed to be by Miss Hook of The Veles, Snodland, now in the ownership of Mr Gerald Edgeler.

PC Israel May of Snodland would have worn a uniform like this one worn by an un-named constable who served at Cranbrook in the 1870s. (Picture: Kent Police Force)

At the time of the murder, Atkins was living on the Snodland side of the river, in a public house owned by William Parker. He had lodged there for seven or eight months before the murder and had lived there, on and off, for several years before that.

He was a big man, nearly six feet tall and heavily built; very fair with a fresh colour in his cheeks and aged 27, although he was described as looking younger. He had a reputation for being a thoroughly bad character: violent, morose and vindictive, although at his trial some witnesses described him as a quiet, well-mannered man.

Atkins and May had crossed paths more than once. When drunk, Atkins was apt to lie down outside the pub or at the side of the road to sleep it off, and more than once he had been woken up by the constable and told to move along.

On at least one occasion when this happened, Atkins was sufficiently angered to utter threats about what he would like to do to May.

Ten days before the murder, at about a quarter to midnight, after being helped aboard the Snodland river ferry by the ferryman, George Gladwell, he complained: 'The . . . bobby hustled me out of the street. I'd like to put a mark on that . . . bobby if I ever got the chance!'

Atkins was drinking at The Bull at Snodland on Saturday night, 23rd August 1873. He was dressed in a monkey jacket, corduroy trousers, a pair of newly-soled boots and a cap.

By about 10.45 pm he was outside the pub, lying on the ground being sick. Two men who knew him tried to help him and got him to his feet. But at that time, PC May came by and, seeing Atkins, he reached out and grabbed him by the coat, pushing him against the wall.

'Are you going home?' the constable asked.

Truculently, Atkins said he was, adding: 'I should like to get you somewhere in the dark!'

The constable was a pretty burly man himself.

'I shouldn't care for a thing like you!' he told the reeling drunk.

With beery bravado, Atkins shouted: 'I don't care for that . . . thing you carry in your pocket,' referring to the constable's truncheon, to which May replied:

'I never have used that and I don't want to now. Get along home with you and stop making a nuisance of yourself.'

At that moment a woman came by. She was making a noise and the constable left Atkins to go and tell her to stop that. Then, he went on his way towards the Snodland turnpike tollgate for a word with the gatekeeper.

Atkins went off with three other men, but after a short distance he could stumble no further and lay down. The other men went on without him.

It was then close to midnight.

At about one o'clock on Sunday morning, the constable was seen on Ham Hill, Snodland, by a Mrs Selina Upton, wife of a beerhouse keeper and lime burner. May wished her goodnight and she knew it was him because, she said afterwards, she saw his buttons shining quite plainly.

At six o'clock the same morning, PC May's body was found, fearfully mutilated, in a turnip field beside the turnpike road leading from Snodland to Malling, some 200 yards from the Snodland turnpike gate.

A Snodland bricklayer called James Stone reached the spot as he walked with a friend towards the neighbouring hamlet of New Hithe. They could see signs that there had been a scuffle of some kind in the road and a man was already looking over the hedge at something in the field.

Stone and his friend went to see what it was and were horrified to find a body lying about six yards from the road. The hedge was, in fact, the boundary between Snodland and the neighbouring parish of Birling and the body was actually on the Birling side of the hedge.

The body was stretched out nearly at full length, with one leg slightly drawn up and an arm stretched out as if to protect the head, which was almost literally shattered to pieces. The other arm was extended full length at his side. Nearby was half of a pair of braces apparently torn from the murderer during the struggle. The ground for some distance round the corpse was covered with blood and signs of the desperate struggle that had taken place.

Stone sent his friend to get the policeman, not realising that they were looking at him, while he himself went to the turnpike gate where the keeper, Mr Furley, returned with him to the scene.

It was Furley who recognised the body as that of PC May and Stone picked up a policeman's hat which he found lying about 18 ft from the body. He also saw a bloodstained cloth cap lying about a yard from the hat and there was a beef sandwich wrapped in paper, a pair of handcuffs and a knife belonging to May at or near the scene, too.

At once a murder investigation was begun, led by Superintendent Hulse of the Malling Division of Kent County Constabulary.

Dr Charles White came and inspected the body. He found the skull was fractured, nose bones broken, several bruises about the head and others elsewhere, all caused by a blunt instrument, except for a bruise at the back of the head which he thought might have been caused by a kick.

He judged that a policeman's staff or truncheon, if wielded by a powerful arm, was such an instrument and, in fact, the truncheon of PC May was missing.

Hulse noted that May's watch had stopped at twenty minutes to three.

The on-the-spot investigations over, May's body was taken to the Bull Inn where, the following day, an inquest was held, at the end of which the Coroner, Mr J. N. Dudlow, found there was not sufficient evidence to determine who was the murderer. The jury returned a verdict of wilful murder against some person or persons unknown.

At the time, though, there was very little doubt in anyone's mind about who was responsible.

The *South Eastern Gazette*, in its report, had no qualms about adding: 'There is, happily, every prospect of the speedy apprehension of the murderer, suspicion pointing pretty clearly to a man who has lately been employed in the neighbourhood as a labourer as the perpetrator of the barbarous deed.

'This man has absconded and it would appear that on Saturday night at 11 o'clock he was heard to threaten the deceased, who had twice been obliged in the course of his duty to remove him from the streets where he was creating a disturbance.

'This man's character seems to have been thoroughly bad – violent, morose, vindictive and there can be but little doubt that he is the criminal.'

The paper also recalled that 'the man's father was tried at Kent Assizes some years ago for the murder of his wife at Malling and was found to be insane.'

Atkins' name was not published at this point, however, and the paper reported surprise that he remained at large a week after the murder, commenting that he had no money with which to travel very far or very fast.

The search for him was thorough and despite the general confidence that the identity of the wanted man was known, other suspects were brought in.

Walter Coste and William Winfield, two privates in the Royal Engineers, were brought before the magistrates at Malling police court having been seen in the neighbourhood during the early hours of the Sunday morning on which May died. They were seen after that in a van travelling towards London and were followed by a constable, who traced them

In Memory of

ISRAEL MAY,

AGED 37 YEARS.

Police Constable of the Malling Division
Kent County Constabulary,
who was found

CRUELLY MURDERED.

On Sunday Morning, August 24th, 1873.

HE RECEIVED A

PUBLIC FUNERAL

On Thursday, August the 28th.

The Memory of the just is Blessed.

*This little memorial card was printed by Kent County Constabulary to com-
memorate the funeral of the first police constable in Kent to be murdered while on
duty.*

to London where they were arrested and brought back to
Malling.

Both protested their innocence of the crime. Coste said he
had been on a Sunday visit to an aunt in Maidstone and that
he and his companion decided they would walk from there
to London. The carrier picked them up and gave them a lift
in his van.

Their stories were checked and the magistrates declared themselves satisfied that the two men were not concerned with the policeman's murder. They were discharged but the murder, although nothing to do with them, was very unlucky for them nevertheless. They were handed over to the military authorities, who took them to Maidstone as deserters from the regiment.

Later that same Tuesday night, Maidstone borough police arrested a man they thought answered the description of the wanted man. Their suspect was found to be wearing a new pair of braces and when they searched the house at which he was staying part of a pair of old braces was found.

However, this incriminating coincidence was satisfactorily explained by the unfortunate man, who was able to prove he had nothing to do with the murder and was released.

Later in the week, on Thursday, another man answering the suspect's description was seen with sundry head wounds. There was not enough evidence to warrant his arrest, but he was put under police surveillance.

Meanwhile, because of Atkin's links with the cement industry, barges on the Medway were searched for stowaways, with no result, and a £1 reward was offered for the discovery of the murdered policeman's truncheon.

That day, Thursday, the funeral of PC May took place in the churchyard of All Saints church at Snodland. The coffin was borne by four policemen and detachments of the force followed, two by two, with crepe armlets, led by Supt Hulse and accompanied by the Chief Constable of Kent, Capt Buxton, and his deputy.

Crowds of local people turned out to watch as the cortege passed through the village. Practically the only person who was not there was the constable's wife. She was forbidden by the police authority to attend 'lest the sight of our universal mourning should prove too much for her.'

The service was conducted by the Rev Canon Carey, who

At least some of these early members of the Kent County Constabulary may have known PC Israel May.
(Picture: Kent Police Force)

lived only about a hundred yards from where the body had been found.

Despite the apparent delay, in fact, Atkins was seen as early as the Tuesday following the murder by two boys and a girl, aged between 11 and 14, who were out gleaning in a field near Birling Lees Wood.

The wood was a large one, covering several miles on the Birling side of the Snodland–Birling boundary. The children saw a man run out of the wood and into another one nearby. After about ten minutes, they saw him again returning to the original cover. They thought he had a handkerchief round his head, which had no cap on it, and the eldest of the children remarked: 'That looks like Tommy Atkins.'

They knew him because they had worked with him locally. But it was not until Thursday that this sighting was reported to the police. At once, Supt Hulse got together all the constables he could muster and sent some of them off to comb the wood on the Birling side, while others were sent into the wood on the Wrotham side.

At about the time the policemen were closing in on him in their pincer movement, early on Saturday morning, Atkins was forced out of cover by hunger. He went to a pub called the Horse and Groom at Stansted to beg for food and was recognised by an ostler who got a message to the police.

As a result, shortly before 8 am on Saturday, Supt Hulse received a telegram from one of his men: 'ATKINS JUST SEEN BY A MAN WHO KNOWS HIM. GONE BY THE HORSE AND GROOM. WE ARE CLOSING UPON HIM. THERE ARE NO MARKS UPON HIM.'

Next, Atkins was seen by a West Malling carrier called Hayes, who plied between there and London. He met up with the fugitive near Kingsdown, going towards London. When he reached Kingsdown, Hayes found PC Euden of the Kent County Constabulary at his home and although the constable had been up all night, he at once followed on Atkins' trail and, shortly afterwards, arrested him.

At about 8.30 am, Supt Hulse received another commendably terse telegram: 'ATKINS APPREHENDED.'

There was no resistance and PC Euden's prisoner was taken to Malling police station where at 11 o'clock the same morning he was charged with the murder of PC May a week before.

After his arrest, Atkins told a constable: 'If it hadn't been for that drink, I wouldn't have been lying there and if May hadn't struck me I shouldn't have struck him.

'He hit me on the head with his staff and knocked me on my knees. I think I must have caught hold of his belt or his coat to save myself from going right down.

'I got up again and he struck at me again and I got hold of

his staff. We struggled together close by the hedge and either went through or over it, I don't know which. I know I was at the bottom.

'We struggled and I got on top. I took the staff away from him and hit him with it on the head five or six times. I then threw the staff away.

'Poor fellow, I didn't think I had served him like that. I didn't think he was dead when I left him and I didn't know he was dead until the Thursday night when I heard three men talking about it as I lay in the hedge.'

In the dock at Malling police court, Atkins trembled slightly as the charge was read to him and it was said he had been three days without food while he was hiding in the wood at Birling.

He remained at Malling police station until Monday morning when he again came before the magistrates, who remanded him to Maidstone gaol. It was later said that during the time he remained there his conduct was quiet and orderly, and when he was committed for trial he was bailed in the sum of £20 and £20 surety.

On the day Atkins was remanded to Maidstone gaol, another man, Thomas Bridger, a 37 year old labourer, was also charged with being an accessory after the fact.

He said he had gone out on Thursday night and found a man without a hat who asked for some food. At first he said he did not know the man but afterwards he admitted he had known him some years before.

He got some bread and cheese and when Atkins asked him if he had heard about the row at Snodland, he said he had and that the constable had been buried that day.

Atkins told him he did not know May was dead.

Bridger pleaded tiredness as his excuse for not telling the police about the meeting and so rendering himself liable to the charge for which he appeared.

Atkins was tried for murder at the Kent Winter Assize on Tuesday, 2nd December 1873. He pleaded not guilty and his defence was that there was no malice aforethought.

At the end of the trial, the jury retired for 15 minutes and then returned a verdict of manslaughter.

Passing sentence, the judge said: 'I would not have anyone go away from this court under the impression that they would be justified in resisting an officer of the police force when lawfully taken into custody.

'But if an officer strikes a man unlawfully and inflicts an injury upon him and then the man, resisting, becomes hot-blooded and causes his death, it is a different matter.

'I cannot doubt that May was attempting to handcuff you when he was not justified in doing so, yet I am compelled to believe that you acted with great violence against him and that before the last of the blows were struck you must have been aware that you were either killing him or committing some serious injuries.

'The consequence is that your offence is a bad one and I must sentence you to 20 years penal servitude.'

The report ended with the words: 'The prisoner heard the sentence with great calmness and was at once removed from the dock.'

An appeal was made by the Rector of Snodland, J Gaspard Le M Carey, for subscriptions to a fund in aid of PC May's widow and her three children.

The appeal began with the words: 'The murder of a police constable is happily an event of rare occurrence; such a thing has never happened before in the county of Kent.

'It needs to be known that his widow is in every way worthy of her devoted husband. She has given proof of an obedience and forebearance during her severe trial which would have graced the greatest lady in the land.'

As well as the widow's fund, a memorial stone was bought, also by public subscription and erected at the place

This simple memorial stone, once surmounted by a cross, in the churchyard of All Saints church, Snodland, is inscribed: In Memory of Israel May, aged 37 years, Police Constable of the Malling Division, Kent County Constabulary. Found cruelly murdered on Sunday morning, August 24 1873. The Memory of the Just is Blessed.

where the murdered constable's body was found. Some time later it was removed to Snodland churchyard where it remains, damaged and without the surmounting cross.

But the words inscribed on the stone are still legible: 'In Memory of Israel May, aged 37 years, Police Constable of the Malling Division, Kent County Constabulary. Found cruelly murdered on Sunday morning, August 24 1873. He received a Public Funeral on Thursday, August 28 1873. The Memory of the Just is Blessed. Erected by Voluntary Contributions.'

63

The Shippe Swallower

★

For its size, few other parts of the United Kingdom have given rise to more news stories, more legends, more tales of tragedy and heroism than that which a medieval writer called, with such perfect aptness, The Shippe Swallower – The Goodwin Sands.

The Goodwins, some ten miles long and about four miles wide, lie roughly six miles off the Deal beach. Legend has it that once they were the fertile island of Lomea, part of the lands owned and fatally neglected by Earl Godwin of Kent, father of that King Harold who lost his life and his throne to the Norman Duke William at Hastings in 1066.

More certainly, they were once part of the land that linked Britain with the European mainland. At low tide they still become firm enough to encourage eccentrics of all kinds to challenge them with games of cricket, football, golf and various other activities of all kinds.

The first recorded cricket match played on the Sands was on Friday, 31st August 1813, when five Ramsgate gentlemen led by Thomas Elgar played four Thanet men led by George Withersden of Bethersden. Withersden's team won by 22 runs to 21. It is probable that tide stopped play!

There was another match in 1824 and in 1839 teams had to be rescued by a passing lugger when a summer storm tossed the sea into such turbulence that it was impossible for the cricketers to leave the 'pitch' in the vessel that had brought them to it.

In 1887, three cyclists rode round the edge of the Sands

and one of them returned with a claim that he had run a mile in three and a half minutes on the Sands.

Four members of the Royal Cinque Ports golf club played a round of golf there on 19th July 1921, which was claimed to be the first time any such thing had been done.

There have been picnics and go-kart races on the Sands, too, but all such fun and games are attended with an element of daring. For when the tide comes in again, the Sands change character completely, with almost malevolent swiftness, transforming from kindly playfellow into a cruelly voracious hazard to shipping of all kinds. Only very seldom in its long history has it reprieved or relinquished any of its victims.

In some parts, the Sands become quicksand, fully deserving the old 'shippe swallower' reputation. But elsewhere their speciality is to hold their victims in a tenacious grip and allow the currents to scour away the sand from bows and stern until the vessel's own weight breaks it up, allowing the sea to despatch the remains with almost uncanny speed and thoroughness.

Many are the stories that are told of the Goodwin Sands: some so bizarre as to be barely credible, some tragic, many of outstanding heroism. Over the years, the Sands are thought to have misered away vast riches in swallowed cargoes and several of their victims are said to still haunt the waters thereabouts.

Long before there were newspapers to carry headlines at all, the reputation of the Goodwin Sands struck terror into the hearts of mariners of all nations.

At least one ship of the Spanish Armada is said to lie beneath the Sands and in the great storm of 1703 no fewer than 13 men-of-war were wrecked there with the loss of 1,300 lives, including that of Admiral Sir Basil Beaumont. The Mayor of Dover was among those who put out from Deal to try to rescue them and, in fact, 270 were saved.

Nevertheless, it was probably the greatest single disaster ever attributed to the Goodwin Sands.

But in another great storm in 1836, of 400 ships anchored for shelter in The Downs, some 250 were driven out of the haven and many of those, too, finished up on the infamous Sands.

Today, technology has blunted their reputation somewhat, but even now ships' masters the world over treat them with respect and steer well clear of them, for they are every bit as capable of demolishing the largest tanker afloat in the 20th century as they were of devouring the smaller vessels of every other century and of any nation that ventured upon their own little realm.

Closely linked with the history of the Sands have been the histories of the Kent coast lifeboats and, before them, the Deal 'hovellers' who performed wonders of seamanship to save lives and salvage cargoes from wrecks.

Nowhere around Britain have lifeboat crews earned a more deserved reputation for sheer courage and consummate seamanship than in the unpredictably tempestuous waters of the English Channel, where they have carried out many hundreds of successful rescues.

One of the ghosts of the Goodwins is the *Lady Lovibond*, which ran aground there in February 1748. She had left London that day with Captain Simon Reed and his new bride, Annetta. They had been married only hours before they sailed, much to the chagrin of the ship's mate, Reed's best friend, who was also in love with Annetta. It was said afterwards that, in blind passion, the mate deliberately wrecked the ship by running it aground on the Sands and, although the weather was calm, the vessel vanished without trace before the very eyes of Deal boatmen hurrying to the rescue.

Another of the ghost ships is the Dover–Ostende paddle steamer *Violet*, which ran aground in a snowstorm in 1857. Only one lifebelt was ever recovered from her as evidence of her total wreck, but she is said to appear from time to time still, eerily churning through the Channel in a determined effort to carry her passengers to safety.

Sometimes, too, storm winds are said to carry with them the pitiful cries of the one woman aboard the Estonian schooner *Toogoo*, lost on 1st November 1919. Deal lifeboatmen were close enough to the vessel to see the crew and the skipper's wife clinging to the rigging, but they could not reach the stricken vessel before she sank beneath a huge wave and was never seen again.

On 1st January 1860, a ship called the *Gutenberg* ran on to the Goodwins in thick fog. Her distress signals were seen at Deal where lifeboatman Stephen Pritchard, knowing another Deal man, Henry Pearson, was aboard as pilot, telegraphed to lifeboatman Stephen Penney at Ramsgate.

The Deal luggers could not launch in the weather conditions but Ramsgate had a steam launch called *Aid* which could tow the lifeboat there into a position from which it could operate effectively.

But when the Ramsgate men applied to the harbourmaster for permission to launch the lifeboat, he refused it because he had not received a signal from either of the Goodwin lightships warning of a vessel in distress.

The harbourmaster was, of course, acting perfectly properly according to the letter of the regulations. But he, like everyone else, knew there was a vessel in distress out there. Despite that, he insisted on waiting for the proper procedure, although every minute that passed made it more likely that the Sands would have their way with the wreck and all who sailed in her.

More urgent telegraphs were sent from Deal but still the Ramsgate harbourmaster refused the vital permission. It was not until three hours later that the South Sand Head lightship spotted the wreck through the fog and fired its signal gun.

Only then would the Ramsgate harbourmaster finally

The Ramsgate tow steamer stands off after taking the lifeboat out to the Aurora Borealis, *aground on the Goodwin Sands, in January 1867.*
(Picture: Kent County Library)

permit the lifeboat to be launched and it was 9.15 before the rescuers at last put out.

It was too late. The lifeboat crew arrived at the scene just in time to hear the dying cries of the last of the 26 crewmen still aboard the wreck. Five had left in a boat and were picked up, but the rest all perished.

Reports of the incident sparked off public anger against the harbourmaster, whose insistence on sticking to the proper routine cost so many lives.

Another memorable wreck was that of the Danish vessel *Aurora Borealis*. She, with her crew of ten, was driven on to the Sands in a snow blizzard on 5th January 1867.

Her signal gun was heard by the crew of the Gull lightship and the Ramsgate lifeboat and its tow steamer put out. Unfortunately, though, they could not locate the wreck in the blinding weather and although they patrolled all through that bitter night in the hope of sighting the vessel at dawn, they eventually had to put back into Margate for a fresh crew.

The new men were more lucky. They found the wreck and after the sort of manoeuvres that lifeboatmen take for granted but which lesser men would dismiss as impossible, they finally threw an anchor aboard the *Aurora Borealis* and got the crew off safely that way.

It was recorded that each lifeboatman in the crew was rewarded by the Board of Trade with £1.1s.0d for that rescue, but the King of Denmark also sent 200 dollars to be shared among them, which worked out at another £3.9s.0d each.

At 2.30 am on 17th December 1872 a signal gun from the Gull lightship sent Coxswain Jarvist Arnold in the Kingsdown lifeboat *Sabrina* and Coxswain William Bushell in Walmer's *Centurian* out into very heavy seas to the aid of the screw steamer *Sorrento* from Newcastle. She had gone aground on the Sands, laden with grain.

The lifeboats found *Sorrento* at the southern end of the Goodwins. They went alongside on a falling tide and while *Centurian* lifeboatmen went aboard to help lighten *Sorrento*'s load, *Sabrina* took out a kedge anchor to prevent the stranded vessel from being driven further on to the Sands.

The Ramsgate boat was towed to the scene but it did not take part in the rescue. It stood by in case extra help was needed.

The Sands had already broken the back of the steamer and the sea was pouring in faster than her pumps could empty it out. The tide was rising and the strength of the gale increased so that the Walmer boat was swept half a mile away before it was brought under control, leaving *Sabrina* to continue alone the rescue of the crew and also of the *Centurian* lifeboatmen who were still aboard.

The lifeboats Sabrina *and* Centurian *carried out a successful rescue of the crew of the Newcastle steamer* Sorrento *which went aground on the Goodwin Sands in 1872.*
(Picture: Kent County Library)

With the men off and all crammed into the one lifeboat, *Sabrina* was too heavy to return without endangering herself and all aboard her by presenting her broadside to the waves. The only alternative was to go straight ahead, across four miles of dangerously broken water over the Sands themselves.

She was followed faithfully by the Walmer boat so that, once clear of the Sands, it could take off some of the rescued men. They were eventually landed safely at Broadstairs, to join that happy band of mariners who have fallen into the clutches of the Goodwin Sands and survived to tell the tale.

A Singular Religious Sect

★

Throughout the 1880s, the Jezreelites in Gillingham were for ever making headlines of one kind or another. Even after the deaths of their leader and his wife, when the Jezreelites themselves faded out of the public eye, for another 70 years the famous landmark on Chatham Hill, known to everyone as Jezreel's Tower, remained a memorial to them and to the mystery man who called himself James Jershom Jezreel.

To this day no-one knows if the name he was using when he first came to public notice in 1875, that of James Rowland White, was his real name. Nor does anyone know where he came from or anything about his family background.

He himself was always reticent, hinting at an upbringing in Roman Catholic France, although there were others who believed he had at least spent some time in America.

It was in the name of James Rowland White, however, that he joined the Army in July 1875 and was posted, a private soldier, to the 2nd Battalion 16th Regiment of Foot at Chatham. There he sought out local disciples of The New House of Israel, a descendant sect of followers of Joanna Southcott. At first he was welcomed and encouraged, and he embraced their teachings so ardently that before long he was a leading member of the church.

But then he declared himself to be the Messenger of the Lord and new leader of the sect. The existing leaders were indignant at that and expelled him summarily. But it was too late. By this time he had attracted many friends upon whom he had made such an impression that they, to a man, abandoned the old leaders and followed him instead.

He announced that he was, in fact, James Jershom Jezreel, he who was sent to lead in fulfilment of the prophecies of Joanna Southcott herself, and to emphasise the break from the past he called his little band The New and Latter House of Israel, to distinguish it from the parent New House of Israel.

It was this still very small group that he left in Gillingham when he was sent with his regiment to India, but not before he had written the Flying Roll, the doctrinal tract of his sect, during a reputed twelve days locked away from all human contact in a closely curtained room.

The Flying Roll was anything but light reading. Many people who did read it found it almost incomprehensible. But all through the six years he was in India it sustained the faithful members of his New and Latter House of Israel, already better-known as Jezreelites, to whom their absent leader sent home further instalments of the doctrine which were later published as twelve sermons.

When his six years abroad were over, Jezreel (he now dropped the name of White altogether) was discharged from the army and he returned to Gillingham where, within a week, he married the daughter of one of his church members, Clarissa Rogers.

She was 21; he claimed to be 32, although there was, as there was with almost everything else about his private life, some doubt about that. He may, in fact, have been older.

The Jezreelites took literally the Biblical commandment against making graven images and banned all pictures except those on coins, so there are no pictures of either Jezreel or his wife.

But from descriptions left by people who knew them both we can say that he was a big, well-built man with piercing eyes and the full beard and long hair that distinguished all men of the sect. He was a man of some personal charm, too: a fluent and persuasive speaker, suave and diplomatic in his dealings with others, with a good sense of humour and a shrewd business instinct. He was very hard-working and frequently spent long night hours studying and book-keeping after a full day's work.

There were stories that made him out to be a drunken lecher, but there was never any real evidence of it and people who knew him spoke of him as 'a perfect gentleman'.

His young wife was smaller, very attractive, somewhat wilful and although she too could work hard and was a good organiser, she was more prone to self-indulgence than he was and was much less popular. She, too, changed her name and was known thereafter as Esther Jezreel.

The Jezreelites lived communally; not all together in one building, but pooling all their possessions into a community chest managed by Jezreel himself, from which he paid all their living expenses, including the rent of the homes they occupied.

The Jezreels themselves lived rather better than most of their followers did. In 1884 they moved into a country house called Woodlands, then on the outskirts of Gillingham, where they began to live in some style, riding about the town in a carriage and pair.

His business acumen put the community money to good use and before long there were Jezreelite shops, owned by the sect and managed by its members, which quickly gained a reputation for fair prices and square dealing. The Jezreelites were generally regarded locally as harmless – indeed, worthy – eccentrics and as such they prospered to a point where there was enough money available to them to prompt Jezreel to go ahead with his dream of building a great headquarters at which Jezreelites from all over the world could gather.

He himself claimed the site for the new building was revealed to him during a morning walk, at the junction of two main roads near the top of Chatham Hill. It was a fine

Jezreel's Tower, as original drawings showed it was intended to look when completed.
(Picture: Kent Messenger archives)

spot with splendid views across the surrounding, then largely rural, countryside, but unfortunately he must have misunderstood the revelation because he found he was unable to acquire the site. However, he was able to buy another one nearby and local architects were engaged to draw up plans.

Jezreel wanted a building that was 144 ft long, broad and high, but he had to bow to practicalities and agree that it should be 124 ft 6 in × 124 ft 6 in × 120 ft high at the corners. He stipulated that it should be of steel and concrete construction, faced with yellow brick on which were to be featured the symbols of the sect: a trumpet and Flying Roll, crossed swords, and the Prince of Wales' feathers to represent The Trinity.

74

The ground floor was to house twelve printing presses which would produce copies of his Flying Roll and other sectarian literature, while on the first floor there was to be a great circular assembly hall able to seat 5,000 people, with galleries round the walls. There would be no windows in this hall, which would be lit by a 45 ft diameter electric lantern in the 94 ft glass dome 100 ft above the floor.

In the space between the square exterior and the circular interior, would be offices, reading rooms and other rooms, and the four corner towers would contain the stairways and lifts up to all floors.

The building was to be lit by both gas and electricity – itself a novelty at the time – and there would be a circular platform in the assembly hall that would rise hydraulically out of the floor and revolve slowly so that a speaker on it could face every one of his audience.

All of this was estimated to cost about £25,000 and wealthy as the Jezreelites now were, they needed more money to complete the work. Messages went out to supporters in America and some sold their homes and businesses and came to Gillingham, where they poured their all into the community coffers. But still the contributions were not arriving quickly enough nor in sufficient quantity.

The work of building the great tower was still not begun when, quite suddenly, on Sunday 2nd March 1885, James Jershom Jezreel died at his home, Woodlands, as a result of breaking a blood vessel.

He had preached his own immortality; indeed, it was one of the sect's central beliefs that true believers would not die but would be translated directly into the hereafter. Some of his followers found the evidence of the error of his teaching too much for their own faith and drifted away, but many more explained his death to their own satisfaction and remained faithful.

The local papers, and some of the national ones, too, all

carried reports of Jezreel's death. As one put it, it was a nine days' wonder and the topic of conversation wherever people gathered together in the Medway towns.

When his funeral was held at Gillingham cemetery on Thursday, 5th March, several thousand curious onlookers gathered at the cemetery gates hoping for a glimpse of strange rites. They were disappointed. The authorities had expected a good deal of interest and barred all but authorised mourners from the scene.

As one Kent journalist reported, they did not miss very much. The funeral was conducted according to Church of England rites and was witnessed by just a few friends – no relatives, of course, except his wife and in-laws – all of whom avoided any show of grief since that would have been to deny their own convictions that their leader was not really dead at all, in the conventional sense, but had only gone ahead of them.

With the leadership vacant, there was a short sharp tussle for succession which Mrs Jezreel won convincingly. With undisputed access to the community assets, she permitted her adherents to refer to her now as Queen Esther and she began to live in relatively regal style, although some of her 'subjects' were in very much straitened circumstances.

She conceived the notion that the Tower her husband had dreamed of should be his memorial and she at once set about getting the work under way.

The corner stone was laid with such ceremony as could be managed on a very wet and windy day in September 1885, and it began to dawn on the locals that the building on Chatham Hill was going to be the biggest church in England, capable of holding more people than St Paul's Cathedral, and a local status symbol of significant prominence.

The building work soon drained the community coffers, however, and the Jezreelite shopkeepers and others were constantly being exhorted to make sacrifices to their late leader's great tower, although it was remarked that Mrs Jezreel – Queen Esther – herself continued to live in the grand manner.

There began to be discontent among the ranks as the building progressed. One man, an American small farmer called Noah Drew, who had sold up and brought his wife and his worldly wealth to the community at Gillingham, tried to sue Mrs Jezreel for his money back. When he lost his case, his solicitors had to sue him for their fee and since he had no money, they tried to recover it from Jezreelite funds, effectively from Mrs Jezreel herself.

They failed in that, too, but shortly afterwards Drew and his wife were evicted from their Jezreelite lodgings, in spite of the fact that the old man barricaded himself in and threatened all comers with an axe.

Some time after the eviction, Drew crossed the path of a Jezreelite procession, complete with band and banner, in the streets of Gillingham and he began denouncing them in public. He soon had a sympathetic audience which turned upon the procession, damaging instruments and tearing the banner to shreds before turning its wrath on nearby Jezreelite property.

Most of the other Americans who could scrape together money for the fare went back to America and the Jezreelite membership dwindled back from perhaps 1,500 to only about 150.

At that low point in the sect's fortunes, Mrs Jezreel developed peritonitis and, at the age of 28, died as suddenly as her husband had. She was buried in the same grave as he was but, significantly, this time only a few hundred people bothered to turn out to watch.

After that it was all downhill for the New and Latter House of Israel. Mrs Jezreel's father, Edward Rogers, assumed the leadership; the name Jezreelites was dropped, and building work on the Tower, which was already at first

The unfinished Tower that became a notable landmark alongside the A2 at Gillingham.
(Picture: Kent Messenger archives)

floor level, was suspended. The builders were owed £6,000 and the only way Rogers could pay the debt was to transfer the title to the building to them and then rent it back, so that the printing that was already going on in the ground floor premises could continue.

But the impetus was lost. In 1905 the remnants of the sect fell behind with the rent of the Tower and the owners repossessed it, intending to convert it into a factory. There were more headlines when the occupying Jezreelites refused to leave when navvies arrived to begin to knock off some of the top bricks in readiness for a roof to be put on the unfinished building.

There was a scuffle, police were called in and the Jezreelites had to stand back and watch the bricks being thrown down to be sold in order to recoup some of the owners' losses.

After that, the Tower remained derelict until 1961, when despite local protest because there was by now considerable affection for the old incomplete building, which had become a unique landmark, it was finally demolished.

The work took 14 months and cost the life of one lorry driver when a hundred tons of masonry fell upon him. Inevitably, perhaps, the rumour spread that the building was protected by the curse of Jezreel.

But at last the work was completed and some of the 6,000 tons of rubble from the site went into the foundations of the new Medway bridge at Rochester, which thus became the new – but completely incognito! – memorial to a remarkable man and what the *South Eastern Gazette* once described as 'a singular religious sect'.

The Bride In The Bath

★

It began, as far as these things can ever be said to begin anywhere in particular, with a chance meeting at Weston super Mare in March 1912.

That was not the first meeting, however. Bessie Mundy had first met the man she knew as Henry Williams in 1910 in Weymouth. Her father had died in 1904 leaving her £2,500, which was transferred into a trust fund from which she received £8 a month. It was a comfortable enough income for a young woman at that time.

When she first met Williams, she thought he was a pleasant sort of man, in his mid 30s, and it was not long before she accepted his proposal of marriage. The couple were married by the Registrar at Weymouth.

Before the wedding, though, Williams had told Bessie he needed money to start a business of his own and he had persuaded her to agree to his asking a Weymouth solicitor to write to her family solicitor requesting copies of her father's will.

At the same time, he wrote on her behalf to her uncle, who controlled the trust, saying that Bessie hoped he would forward as much money as possible.

The uncle was not altogether happy about the request, but Bessie was fully entitled to draw money from the fund and so a cheque for £135.2s.11d was sent to the happy couple.

No sooner was the cheque cashed and the money safe in Williams' pocket than he told his bride, in the most forthright terms, that she had injured his health and he had to go away for treatment.

The conventions of the time forebade any more specific reference to his accusation afterwards, but now it can be said that he claimed he had contracted a venereal disease and that he blamed her for it. He said he had to go to London for treatment and it might be some months before he was cured.

'You had better tell your uncle you had the money in your handbag when you fell asleep on the beach and lost it,' he told her. 'Otherwise, there will be police proceedings and you and your family will be publicly disgraced.'

Then, leaving her to pay the rent for their lodgings, he went out of her life. She did not know it, but he actually went back to a woman called Edith Pegler, who he had 'married' in Bristol before he met Bessie, despite the fact that he was, even then, legally married to Caroline Thornhill, from whom he had parted in 1905.

Bessie, shocked and distressed by his behaviour, turned to her brother, George, who invited her to stay with him, which she did for two or three months.

That might have been that. She had lost touch with her 'husband' and was resigned to the fact that she would never see him again. Slowly, she recovered from the experience, resumed her independent life, and two years later was living in Weston super Mare when who should she bump into, quite by chance, but the man she still supposed was her husband, Henry Williams.

It was that reunion that sealed the fate of poor Bessie Mundy and made her one of the most celebrated victims in the annals of English criminology.

But when they met, she was pleased to see him again. Within hours of the meeting, she was speaking of him in public in the most affectionate terms, introducing him to friends and acquaintances as her husband, and soon he was writing to her brother, George Mundy, saying Bessie was reunited with her husband and that no husband could possibly be more sorry than he was for what had occurred in the past.

'Time is a great healer,' he wrote. 'Bessie and I are living together again and she has told her friends she is delighted to be with me once more.'

This time, the couple went to live in Herne Bay in Kent, where they rented a small house at 80 High Street, and furnished it very cheaply from local shops.

One of their purchases was a bath – a zinc bath about five feet long, with four legs – which was installed in the only bedroom in the house. The bath would have cost them £1.17s.6d after Williams had haggled the price down from £2, if he had not taken it 'on approval' before parting with any money at all for it!

In Herne Bay, Williams represented himself as an antiques and art dealer and he and Bessie both made wills in each other's favour, each leaving everything to the other. In fact, he had virtually nothing to leave and although Bessie understood that, it did not seem to bother her. Legally, as his wife, all that was hers became his anyway.

With the ink barely dry on the wills, Williams took his wife to see a local doctor, Dr French, saying she had had some kind of fit. Bessie had no recollection of it and seemed to the doctor to be in good health, but later that same week, Williams sent for the doctor to come to the house where he was told Mrs Williams had suffered another fit.

Again, there was no obvious evidence of it, although Bessie confessed she did have a headache, and Dr French, supposing he had another hypochondriac couple on his list of patients, advised rest and went away.

Just after eight o'clock on the morning of 13th July, Dr French received a note from Williams. It said simply: 'Can you come at once. I am afraid my wife is dead.'

When Dr French arrived at the house, he found Williams in a downstairs room. Together, they went upstairs, where they saw the body of Bessie lying, face up, in the bath full of water. Her feet were resting on the rim of the foot of the bath, which was about eight inches shorter than she was. The rest of her body, including her mouth, was under the water.

Williams told the doctor he and his wife had both got up at about 7.30 that morning and he had left the house to buy some fish. When he returned, he said, he found his wife as she was now.

The story required its listeners to believe that Bessie, who was supposed to be suffering from fits, had made about 20 journeys up the stairs with buckets of hot water in order to fill the bath, and had got herself into it in the time between getting out of bed at about 7.30 and the time her husband found her and wrote the note that reached the doctor at soon after 8 am.

Dr French was also surprised that a woman who had had a fit in her bath should have finished up in the position in which she was found.

Nevertheless, an inquest returned a verdict of death by misadventure and Bessie was duly buried.

Although the phrase was not to come into sensational use until much later, Bessie Mundy had become the first of the Brides in the Baths victims of murderer George Joseph Smith.

For Henry Williams was not the real name of the man she believed she was legally married to. Before he was brought to justice, he used a number of aliases, including Love, Smith, Williams, Lloyd and James. He 'married' at least seven women, of whom Bessie was the third, and although three of them, including Bessie, died in their baths (the others lived), he was eventually tried only for the murder of Bessie, his first known victim.

Bessie Mundy's family was suspicious about the circumstances of her death, but could not prevent her 'husband' inheriting her property under the terms of the will she had made in his favour.

R. AUGUST 14, 1915

THE WAR.

COUNTY EDITION.

SMITH EXECUTED
AT MAIDSTONE

THIS MORNING.

What Happened ?

The "Brides in the Baths" Case.

Smith, the villain of the "brides in the baths" dramas, paid the penalty of his crimes this (Friday) morning when, at eight o'clock, he was hanged in Maidstone Prison.

The condemned man, since his removal to Maidstone on Wednesday week, had been visited several times daily by the Rev J. Stott, one of the Bishop of Southwark's ablest missioners, who has been acting as Chaplain in the absence of the Rev. E. Stephens, who is with the troops at the front.

The Rev. R J. Wardell, Wesleyan Minister of Maidstone, has also visited the culprit, who claimed to belong to the Wesleyan Methodist persuasion

We understand that Smith welcomed the ministrations of both these gentlemen, and that during the last few days of his life he appeared to be in a penitent frame of mind.

The usual officials were present at the execution, but for the first time for many years for no particular reason that we can gather—the representatives of the Press were excluded, so that, from the public point of view, the arrangements for the execution were not so satisfactory as has been the case hitherto in the County Town.

A couple of London Press photographers arrived in Maidstone on Thursday afternoon, and one of them at once proceeded up the County Road to take a snap-shot of the entrance to the Gaol. He had scarcely got to work when a constable made his appearance and requested him to accompany him to the Police Station, where he was informed that as Maidstone was a prohibited area, it was an offence to take a snapshot of any of the buildings.

Both photographers returned to London without any pictures.

The Last Scene.

It was a brilliantly fine morning—one of the few brilliant mornings of this summer—

Latest War News.

The latest news from the Russian front shows that not only is Hindenburg's great north movement making no progress at present, but in the bend of the front west of Dwinsk our Allies are pressing back the enemy, the civil population is leaving Dwinsk.

H.M. auxiliary cruiser India (Commander W G. A. Kennedy, R.N.), whilst engaged on patrol duty in the North Sea on August ... was torpedoed by a German submarine and sunk. Twenty-two officers and 119 men have been saved.

The Vice-Admiral in the Dardanelles reports that one of the British submarines operating in these waters sank a Turkish battleship on the morning of August 8th at the entrance to the Sea of Marmora. A Turkish gunboat, the Berk-i-Satvet, and an empty transport have also been torpedoed in the Dardanelles by one of the British submarines.

Naval, military and civic honours were paid to the memory of the late Flight Sub-Lieut at his funeral yesterday at Chatham. The body was carried on a gun-carriage to the cemetery by a naval detachment from Chatham. Naval pipers played their laments and the coffin was shrouded by the Union Jack. From the church to the cemetery the body was borne to the graveside by officers of the Royal Flying Corps, and lieutenants of the deceased provided for the coffin. His mother and father were among the family mourners.

Affray at Detling Ca...

At the Bearsted Magistrates Court, Maidstone, on Tuesday, Alfred ... son, a canteen attendant at the camp, Detling, was charged with inflicting bodily harm upon Wm. Adams ... Garrett stated that at 1.30 that ... was called to the Junior Army and Navy Stores' tent at Detling Camp, ... prosecutor lying on a bed suffering from compound fracture of the right jaw and injuries to his face. The man said the prisoner had struck him with an iron. Witness arrested the accused, who in reply to the charge: "No, I ... did it with my fist."—On the charge the prisoner was remanded by the ... J. Barker)till Monday.

KENT AND THE N...
REGISTE...

NOTABLE VOLUNTARY

The country is in the throes of Registration, and in this ...

84

Williams told his landlady his wife must have had another fit while she was taking a bath.

'I found her dead in the bath,' he said, adding with what was even then regarded as very poor taste and was later seen to have more sinister import: 'Wasn't it a jolly good job I got her to make a will?'

He returned the bath to the shop he had got it from, sold the furniture and gave up the house at Herne Bay. Then he wrote to Edith Pegler, asking her to join him in Kent, where they spent two months together in Margate before he left her again.

He drew out 14 cheques for large sums of money from his inheritance and bought seven houses in Bristol for £2,180. He later sold six of them for £1,365.

In the next three years, he married four more times. Two of those 'wives', Alice Burham, who died at Blackpool on 12th December 1913 and Margaret Lofty (Highgate, 18th December 1914), died in their baths. It was stretching co-incidence too far and in June 1915, in the name of George Joseph Smith, he was charged with murdering Beatrice Constance Annie Mundy at Herne Bay on 13th July 1912.

He was then 43 years old.

The Old Bailey trial lasted nine days, at the end of which the judge said there was no direct evidence that Smith had murdered Mundy, nor that he was present in the bathroom when she died.

Evidence was given, however, that the simplest way to drown someone in a bath was to pull the feet forward and hold them there, making it impossible for the victim to struggle free.

In his summing up, the judge, Mr Justice Scrutton, described the murder as a cold-blooded and heartless crime and the murderer as a man on whom exhortations of repentance would be wasted.

Smith interrupted several times with such comments as:

Maidstone Prison still looks now as it did the day George Joseph Smith was hanged there.

'You might as well hang me today' and: 'I am no murderer, though I may be a bit peculiar.'

The jury retired at eight minutes to three in the afternoon of 1st July and returned at ten minutes past three with a 'guilty' verdict.

Asked if he had anything to say, Smith replied: 'I can only say I am not guilty.'

He was sentenced to be executed at Maidstone prison and after an appeal had failed, the sentence was duly carried out at eight o'clock in the morning of Friday, 13th August 1915.

A local newspaper reporter recorded that it was one of the few really fine days of that summer. There were other singularities about the execution, too.

A *Kent Messenger* journalist reported: 'For the first time for many years – for no particular reason that we can gather –

the representatives of the Press were excluded; so that from the public point of view the arrangements for the execution were not so satisfactory as has been the case hitherto in the County Town.'

Another departure from normal procedure was that the Press was not notified of the inquest and those who found out about it were not permitted to view the body.

Again, the *Kent Messenger*: 'No explanation of this refusal was offered. What happened at the execution to make it inadvisable that the body should be seen as usual?'

London Press photographers who arrived to take pictures outside the gaol were taken by policemen to Maidstone police station, where they were told Maidstone was a war-time prohibited area and it was an offence to take pictures of any building there. The Pressmen returned to London without their pictures.

When the execution was over, the break with tradition was continued. There was no traditional tolling of the prison bell and no hoisting of the equally traditional black flag over the prison to tell the public gathered at the prison gates that the deed was done, and that George Joseph Smith, described by one journalist as 'one of the greatest criminals of the century', had followed his Brides in the Baths into the criminal history books.

Fire!

A major fire, wherever it occurs, is always good 'copy' for journalists. When the fire engulfs a familiar landmark, such as the local Big House, and involves elements of tragedy and mystery, it is bound to make headline news.

Such was the fire at The Hall in Wateringbury, a river Medway-side village a short distance out of Maidstone on the Tonbridge road.

The fire broke out at about midnight on Monday, 17th October 1927 and it wiped out the Bazley-White family who lived there: Capt Richard Booth Leslie Bazley-White, DSO, Royal West Kent Regiment and Egyptian Army, his wife Katherine and their four year old son, John.

It also claimed the life of John's nurse, 55 year old Miss Rose Weekes, whose home was at Bearsted on the other side of Maidstone.

So much for the tragedy.

The Hall was a rambling old-fashioned Tudor house near Mereworth Castle, just off the Tonbridge Road. The family had lived there for about 18 months, having previously lived at Boxley, another village to the north of Maidstone.

There were seven people sleeping in The Hall that Monday night and part of the mystery was why the family and the nurse perished in the fire when servants who were sleeping on the same floor of the building escaped. Nor was it ever established quite how or even where the fire started.

The family and the servants were in their rooms by about 10.30 that night. Some of the servants afterwards said they

Kent Messenger *headlines on Saturday, 22nd October 1927.*

spent some time in their rooms reading or writing letters by
candlelight and it was said that the Captain and two of the
maids smoked.

Possibly more relevant was the fact that there had been
fires during the day in both the study and the day nursery,
but as far as anyone knew, nowhere else upstairs.

The Captain was probably the last to go to his room. He
left the gas-lit study where the house telephone was and
went to his wife's bedroom at the back of the house, on the
first floor, to bid her goodnight, as was his habit. After that,
he retired to his own room on the same floor.

It was about 12.15 am when the cook, a widow named Mrs
Edith Whitfield, was woken up by the sound of Mrs Bazley-
White shouting: 'FIRE!' She was running up and down the
steps between the two women's bedrooms.

When Mrs Whitfield opened her bedroom door, intending
to go down to the study and use the telephone to call the fire

89

Captain Richard Booth Leslie Bazley-White, DSO, of the Royal West Kent Regiment and Egyptian Army.

brigade, she saw flames and smoke coming through the open study door. She ran back to her own room, closed the door, and, opening her window, sat on the ledge, shouting 'FIRE!' out into the night before she launched herself out and down on to the gravel path below. Then she ran round the house, still shouting the alarm.

After a minute or two, she set off for her father's home, which was only about 300 yards away, shouting 'FIRE!' as loudly as she could all the way. By the time she reached the house, she was close to collapse but she woke up her father and three brothers, one of whom, Ben, gathered up some sheets and set off at once on his motor bike for the burning house.

Parlourmaid Marjorie Sharp was also woken by Mrs Bazley-White's screams. She flung on a coat over her night clothes and escaped from the house by the back stairs. Mrs Bazley-White could have done the same if she had left at the same time. But if, as seems likely, she went along the corridor to the night nursery where her son and the nurse both slept, by the time she turned back towards the stairs that escape route would have been cut off and the three of them would have been trapped at that end of the corridor, with Capt Bazley-White in his room.

The cook's father, Stephen Butcher, awakened by his daughter, ran from his house towards the burning Hall. As he did so, he saw a taxi coming towards him from nearby Mereworth, and he stopped it. Told about the fire, the driver said he was going to Maidstone, but he volunteered to find a telephone and call for help.

The taxi-driver was 20 year old Frank Franklin of Maidstone. He had taken a fare from Maidstone to Tonbridge and was returning at about 12.45 am when he was stopped by Butcher. He could see the fire, so he went straight to the house of the police sergeant at Wateringbury.

But when he got there his hammering on the door had no

effect. He could not make anyone hear and he afterwards learned that the sergeant was, in fact, away from home.

While he was there, though, Franklin was joined by a friend of his called Charles Pearce.

'I'll try the railway station signal box,' Pearce suggested, and he clambered over the nearby railway fence in order to shout up to the signalman.

'There's a fire at The Hall! Phone for the fire brigade, quick!'

The signalman was not to be ordered about like that, however.

'You'll have to go to the police sergeant's house,' he told Pearce. 'I'm not authorised to make phone calls just like that.'

Pearce controlled his impatience.

'We've already tried the sergeant's house. We can't get any reply.'

The signalman was unimpressed.

'Well, I can't make the call from here,' he insisted. 'On whose authority would I make it? And who would pay for the call? Besides, the fire brigade wouldn't come out if I did call them.'

Pearce and Franklin decided they were wasting precious time. Franklin turned away and ran across the road to the public house, leaving Pearce to tell the signalman what he thought of him.

'You're a silly old fool!' he shouted as he, too, turned away – a remark which, when it was reported at the inquest, drew from the Coroner the comment: 'I do not think that was an over-statement, in the circumstances.'

Meanwhile, Franklin had hammered on the pub door, again without getting any response and, desperate now, he went next to the home of Dr Severne.

It was by then about five minutes past one and the fire at The Hall had been raging for about an hour.

The doctor was, perhaps, more used to being knocked up in the middle of the night. He came down to see what was the matter and, when he heard the story, he hurried off to make the vital phone call while the taxi-driver and his friend, Pearce, hurried back to The Hall. There they found that the whole of the back of the house was now alight.

Climbing a standpipe, Franklin managed to look through the window of the room he was told was Mrs Bazley-White's. The room was lit by flames but the bed was empty, the bedclothes tossed back. The door to the room was closed but there seemed to be no-one in it.

By now hot slates were beginning to slide off the roof all about the would-be rescuer and he slid back down the standpipe and ran round to the other side of the building, where the maids' rooms were.

That part of the house was a mass of flames, so he abandoned any hope of reaching anyone who might be inside and instead ran to his taxi to get a tyre lever, with which he broke open the front door of the house and went inside to see if there was anything he could salvage before the fire got to it.

The main staircase was not burning and, hearing sounds that he afterwards described as 'like the groans of an old lady' he went upstairs. There, a mass of flames was shooting along the corridor and he heard what he thought was a gun being fired before he was beaten back by the heat of the fire and he had to return downstairs to rejoin the others.

The long delayed telephone call finally reached Maidstone Fire Brigade at 1.10 am and the firemen were on the scene by 1.27 am. Fire Chief William Wainscot said he was told on arrival that there was no-one in the house.

Subsequent investigation led him to believe the fire had started on the first floor and burned downwards. He thought it started in the Captain's room because that was where the fire was burning most fiercely when he arrived.

Mrs Katherine Bazley-White.

It took the firemen until about five o'clock that morning to get the blaze under control. Then they were able to dig out the body of Mrs Bazley-White, which they found lying on the drawing room floor.

A further search discovered the Captain's body, buried beneath debris, and later the body of the nurse, Miss

Weekes, was also found, lying almost on top of the child, the remains of a bed frame underneath them both.

At the inquest, the Coroner and the fire chief disagreed about exactly where the fire had started and so provided one of the elements of mystery that surrounded the fire at Wateringbury Hall.

The Coroner plumped for the study, and the jury agreed with him. The fire chief, however, thought it had started in the Captain's bedroom.

The Coroner said he saw no reason to believe the Captain ever woke up from his sleep. He preferred to believe the nurse had been bending over the child's cot, presumably intending to pick him up, when she and he had fallen through the burning floor into the room below.

The fire chief begged to differ over that, too. He believed the Captain had got out of bed, fallen to the floor, where he may have partially recovered and groaned – the sound the taxi-driver said he heard before he came up the stairs.

He thought the nurse must have taken the child from the night nursery into the adjoining Captain's room, where Mrs Bazley-White had already roused her husband. There, all four of them had been overcome by smoke and fallen through the floor into the room below.

That, said Fire Chief Wainscot, was the only reasonable explanation for the positions in which the bodies were found.

According to that theory, it must have been the Captain's bed that Miss Weekes collapsed on to and not the child's cot, as the Coroner's conclusion suggested. Either that, or she had suffocated in her sleep, without ever leaving her own bed which went through the floor with her still in it, perhaps tipping her out and partly over the body of the child who, in that case, must have fallen, still in his cot, a few moments before. All four victims were said to have died of smoke suffocation.

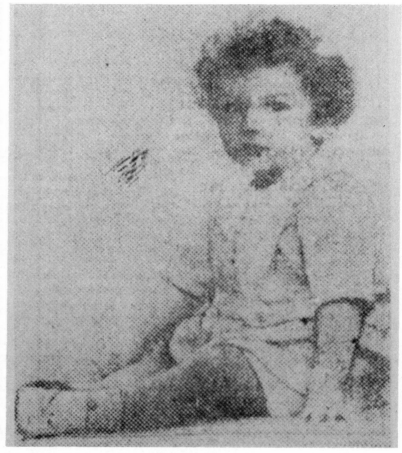

Four year old John Bazley-White, who also died in the fire at the family home.

The one common assumption was that Mrs Bazley-White, who seemed to have been the first person in the house to become aware of the fire, could have escaped if she had not braved the flames and gone to rouse her husband and save her little boy. Perhaps, after all, it was she who took the child from his cot – if, in fact, anyone did – and ran with him into her husband's room, leaving the nurse still asleep in her own bed.

Why she, and for that matter her husband and the nurse as well as the boy, were not able to escape through the very large windows only some ten feet from the ground, was never explained. Two of the servants did just that, although the housemaid, Olive Selves, had hung in her nightdress from a window ledge for some moments before she found the courage or the desperation needed to allow her to drop to safety.

There was one more mystery that was never conclusively explained, too. Also retrieved from the debris left by the fire were two hand-guns: a Webley service weapon and an automatic. The Webley had apparently not been used recently, but the other one had been fully loaded with six bullets, one of which had melted in the chamber in the heat of the fire and three had exploded. The remaining two were intact.

No evidence was given at the inquest that suggested anyone had deliberately fired the gun, but a number of questions that might have been asked about it were not asked, and the conclusion that was reached was that the shots Franklin heard had, in fact, been ammunition, including the three spent bullets in the loaded gun, exploding in the heat.

We shall never know for sure. The only people who could have told us were the Captain and his lady and they both died in the fire at Wateringbury Hall.

Imperial Chislehurst

★

The funeral cortege that crossed Chislehurst Common on 11th July 1879 was the most magnificent ever seen in the little West Kent town.

Thousands of people lined the route of the procession, which included representatives of European Royalty and was watched by Queen Victoria herself, as the last pretender to the title of Emperor Napoleon of France was carried from the exiled family's home at Camden Place to the Roman Catholic church of St Mary.

The death of the Prince Imperial was an occasion of genuine sadness in Chislehurst. The townsfolk had shared the grief of the Empress Eugenie when his father, the Emperor Napoleon III, died six years before, in January 1873. But now they grieved for a man they regarded not just as a welcomed exile but as one of their own; someone who had grown up among them and who shared fully in the respect and affection the whole family received from the local people.

The association between Chislehurst and the Napoleonic dynasty had begun 40 years before, when Prince Louis Napoleon (later Napoleon III) was a young man, in the 1830s.

He was the third son of Louis Bonaparte, King of Holland and therefore nephew of that Napoleon I who changed the course of history and who declared himself Emperor of France in 1804. After the Battle of Waterloo in 1815, Napoleon abdicated his title in favour of his son and, when he in turn died in 1832, Prince Louis Napoleon became head of the Napoleonic dynasty.

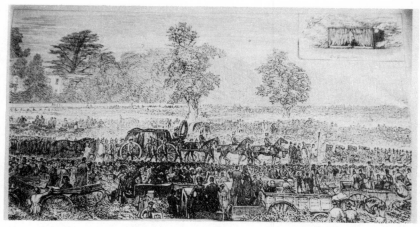

Part of the funeral procession that carried the body of the Prince Imperial, Prince Louis Napoleon, crossing Chislehurst Common on the way to the church.
(Inset: The specially constructed alcove from which Queen Victoria watched the procession)

It was in London during the 1830s that the exiled Prince first met young Emily Rowles. She was a noted beauty, and daughter of Henry Rowles who was distinguished for, among other things, having built Drury Lane Theatre. Emily was born at Camden Place in Chislehurst and was not yet out of her teens when she attracted the eye and, it seems, captured the heart of the Prince, who became a fairly frequent visitor to her home in Chislehurst.

But the Prince had ambitions to revive the family fame and fortunes in France and in 1840 he decided the time was right to make his bid to proclaim himself the rightful heir of his illustrious forebear. With a small party of loyal supporters, he sailed from England to Boulogne where he fully expected to be welcomed rapturously by enthusiastic compatriots.

In fact, however, his reading of the situation and the advice of his supporters proved to be faulty. Instead of the welcome he so confidently expected as he stepped ashore, he was promptly arrested and tucked away, a prisoner, in the castle of Ham on the river Somme.

There he remained for six years, during which time his faithful Emily continued to write to him and send him comfort parcels, even after her own father committed suicide, her mother remarried and they all went to live in Florence.

Quite how much the princely prisoner needed comfort, in parcels or any other form, may be questioned since his time in captivity brought him two sons by a certain Mlle Vergeot. Nevertheless, the parcels duly reached him and although there can be no certainty about it, it is likely that it was one of them – or possibly a discreet series of them – that contained the workman's clothes in which the Prince was eventually able to disguise himself and escape from the castle in 1846.

He made his way across the French border into Belgium and so returned to London, leaving his sons with their mother in the castle. His relationship with Emily Rowles ended after that, but the Prince was soon directing his attentions towards another young lady of considerable beauty called Elizabeth Howard (or Haryett), who had already had a son and a very handsome settlement from one Major Martin of the Guards.

Her fortune, which increased rapidly as her investments in some of the most fashionable parts of London became ever more valuable, was handled by a trustee who, by a strange coincidence, was Mr Nathaniel William Strode of Chislehurst.

Despite the Prince's experiences, he still harboured political ambitions in France and he was no doubt sustained financially, probably substantially, by Miss Howard's generosity, either for personal reasons or because Mr Strode regarded the Prince and his aspirations as a good investment and advised her accordingly.

When King Louis Philippe, the Citizen King of France,

abdicated and fled to England after the revolution of 1848, Prince Louis Napoleon once more launched himself into his country's political arena and this time he won election as a Deputy in the Constituent Assembly of the Second French Republic.

By the end of the year he had been elected President of the Assembly and in 1852 he headed a successful coup and declared himself Emperor. This time, France was with him. A plebiscite was held and he was confirmed in the title by a massive majority. On 2nd December 1852, he was installed at the Tuileries as Emperor Napoleon III and so launched the Second French Empire.

Back in England, Miss Howard must have watched his progress with very mixed feelings. There would have been some pride in the knowledge that she had played such a generous part in her handsome Prince's achievements, but she would have known, too, that as Emperor there could be no place for her in his life any more.

The new Emperor needed a wife and Empress and he found yet another very beautiful woman to fill the role in Maria Eugenia Guzman y Palafox y Porto Carrero, Countess of Teba and Mora, Duchess of Penaranda, second daughter of the Count of Montijo. Not surprisingly, history was to know her better as simply the Empress Eugenie.

Miss Howard was respectably married in London and retired to the Chateau de Beauregard not far from Paris where she lived with her own son by the Major and also the two sons of the Emperor by Mlle Vergeot, until her death in 1865.

The principal witness at her wedding was her trustee, Mr Strode, who had bought Camden Place in 1860 and spent a great deal of money converting it into a typically French chateau.

Quite why he did that we do not know. He may just have admired all things French. If he had foreseen the rise of the

Prince and inspired Miss Howard's backing for it, perhaps he also now foresaw the fall of the Emperor and prepared to capitalise on that, too.

Whatever the truth of it, he certainly received 900,000 French francs from the Emperor out of the French Civil List, which was either a thank-you gift for services rendered or repayment of what the Emperor regarded as a loan from Miss Howard.

The Second French Empire began, as have so many new regimes throughout history, with considerable promise and the Emperor embarked upon a programme of public works that cleared the worst of the slums of Paris and made it the foremost capital of Europe. He sided with the British in the Crimean War, at the end of which he and Eugenie paid a state visit to England and stayed with Queen Victoria at Windsor. It was the beginning of a very real and lasting friendship between the Queen and the Empress.

The downfall of the Second Empire began with the Franco-Prussian War in 1870. Much had changed since Napoleon I led the French Army to so many glories and this campaign was ill-timed and ill-omened. Six weeks after the declaration of war, Napoleon lost the decisive Battle of Sedan and surrendered himself and his army, though not before he had despatched his 14 year old son Louis, the Prince Imperial, to England via Belgium.

The Empress, who was left behind in Paris to act as Regent during her husband's absence at war, had to face the abrupt reversal of public opinion alone. Mobs of Parisians who had cheered the army when it marched out, now turned in wrath upon the gates of the Tuileries. Some of her advisers urged her to 'feed' the malcontents with lead shot, but she could not bring herself to shed more blood. The Prussians were, in any case, advancing to lay siege to Paris and she undoubtedly did the wisest thing when she slipped away from the Palace in disguise and made her way to that ever-welcoming haven for exiles, England.

She landed at Ryde on the Isle of Wight and from there she went to Hastings where she met the Prince Imperial.

Mr Strode lost no time in offering them both the hospitality of his home, Camden Place at Chislehurst, and as soon as the Empress saw it she felt so much at home there that she accepted the offer at once. She and the Prince took up residence there on 20th September 1870.

The Emperor, meanwhile, did not abdicate, so the Empress remained his Regent, although in exile. When Napoleon was released in March 1871, the good news was carried to her at Camden House by the station master at Chislehurst, a Mr Lord, and she went at once to Dover where her own welcome was endorsed by the cheers of the crowds who gathered to see him land.

Camden House now became the headquarters of Imperial France in exile, although in France itself the Third Republic was declared. It is said that the new regime posted spies at the top of Chislehurst windmill from where they could watch and report upon all the comings and goings at Camden Place, while the Emperor posted his own spy at the bottom of the same windmill to spy on the spies at the top!

So it was that the little town became Imperial Chislehurst. The tricolour flew over Camden Place and the Imperial Family entered as fully as they were able to into local life, responding with great generosity to appeals by local charities. The Emperor even tried to understand cricket and watched many a game on the Common.

Not surprisingly, the family was treated with respect and some warmth by the local people. The personal friendship of Queen Victoria for Empress Eugenie brought Her Majesty to Camden Place on several occasions and when Napoleon III died there on 9th January, 1873, the Queen paid for the granite sarcophagus that was erected in the mausoleum the Empress had built on to St Mary's Roman Catholic church.

The funeral was a handsome one and certainly the most spectacular that Chislehurst had witnessed up to that time.

The mortuary chapel at Chislehurst church where the Prince Imperial and his father were buried.

The hearse was drawn by eight horses caparisoned in black and the cortege took half an hour to cross the Common to the church.

The following year, the Prince Imperial celebrated his coming of age at Chislehurst, in March 1874, and several thousand French Bonapartists gathered in marquees set up in the grounds for the occasion. Most of them believed – or for various reasons professed to believe – that the Prince would one day inaugurate the Third Empire.

But the Prince himself had different ambitions. He wanted a commission in the British Army so that he could go with friends from the Royal Military Academy at Woolwich to the war in Zululand.

The Army, however, ruled that out of the question and the Prince finally had to be satisfied with being allowed to accompany his friends as an observer only. He was permitted to wear British officer's uniform, but he had no rank in the British Army to go with it.

So it was that the last of the Napoleonic dynasty fulfilled the family destiny to die on alien soil. Not one of them died in France. Napoleon I ended his days a prisoner on the island of St Helena; his son, Napoleon II never actually reigned and spent most of his adult life in Austria; Napoleon III was buried at Chislehurst, where he died.

Now his son ended the family tradition in far-off Africa. *The Times* reported what happened. The Prince went with a party under the command of Lieutenant Carey from the Army's Quartermaster-General's Department to find a new camp site. He had laughed at objections to his joining the expedition and refused to listen to advice that it would be better if he did not do so.

The party arrived at what they decided would be a suitable place by the Inyolozi river and there they unsaddled their horses to rest for an hour, thinking themselves safe from Zulu attack.

But while they rested, they suddenly found themselves surrounded by Zulu warriors. Quickly, they mounted up – all except the Prince, who had some kind of difficulty resaddling his horse and was left behind with only his service revolver for defence.

When the war was over, Zulus recalled the incident and said he fought bravely and died, speared to death, facing his attackers.

When the rest of the party returned to the main force to

report the Prince's fate, General Marshall himself at once set out with a body of cavalry to the spot where the Prince had fallen. The Zulus fled, leaving the body stripped of its clothing but not of the necklet and locket round the neck. That had been left as a tribute to a brave enemy.

When the news reached England, Queen Victoria telegraphed her sympathy to Eugenie, who was reported to have sunk into a senseless stupor when told the sad tidings by the Lord Lieutenant of Kent, Earl Sydney.

As a result of the incident, Lt Carey was court martialled and charged with 'indiscretion'. He would have faced the death penalty but the Empress herself asked for that sentence to be quashed, saying that it would achieve nothing more than yet another widow. The lieutenant was returned to duty.

The funeral of Prince Louis Napoleon took place on Saturday, 11th July 1879 at Chislehurst. The Admiralty yacht *Enchantress*, with the body on board, came up the Thames to Woolwich the day before and the coffin was carried by sailors to the Armoury, where it was received by about 300 French officials and formally identified.

After that, the coffin was placed on a gun carriage drawn by eight horses and, headed by a squadron of Royal Artillery and followed by mourners on foot and in carriages, the procession set off for Chislehurst.

The band of the Royal Artillery played Beethoven's Funeral March and minute guns were fired from the artillery park at the western end of the Barracks Parade. The Prince of Wales and the Dukes of Edinburgh, Connaught and Cambridge were present for part of the ceremonial.

It took the procession nearly two hours to reach Chislehurst, where all the principal shops were closed and the whole seven-mile funeral route was crowded with spectators – some estimates put the crowd at ten thousand.

On Saturday morning, Queen Victoria and Princess Beatrice left Windsor Castle for Chislehurst at nine o'clock. The Queen went to the Chapelle Ardente where the late Prince lay and there Her Majesty and the Princess laid a wreath of laurels and a cross of flowers on the coffin. The Royal couple spent some time with the Empress Eugenie before returning to Windsor.

The funeral pall was borne by the Prince of Wales (later, of course, King Edward VII), the Duke of Edinburgh, the Duke of Connaught, Prince Leopold, the Crown Prince of Sweden and Norway and the Duke of Cambridge, and the procession from Camden House to St Mary's church, headed by military cadets from Woolwich, included all the most distinguished of the French Bonapartists and deputations from towns and villages throughout France.

After that, the Empress lived on at Camden Place alone for a time. A monument to the Prince was erected by public subscription in 1881 on Chislehurst Common, near Prince Imperial Road, and Queen Victoria erected a monument to the Prince in St George's Chapel, Windsor. Royal Artillery officers and cadets erected another at the Royal Military Academy at Woolwich, which was later removed with the Academy itself to Sandhurst.

Unable to enlarge St Mary's church at Chislehurst as she would have liked to, Eugenie built St Michael's Abbey at Farnborough, Hants, and in March 1881 she left Chislehurst, where she had lived for eleven years, for her new home in Hampshire. The bodies of both the Emperor Napoleon III and the Prince Imperial were removed to the abbey on 9th January 1888 and Eugenie finally joined them after she died in Madrid on 11th July, 1920.

Today, Chislehurst is part of the London Borough of Bromley, although still in the Kent postal area. Camden Place is now the club house of Chislehurst Golf Club.

But the memories linger on. One of the last significant reminders of Chislehurst's Imperial past vanished when three figures replaced the old Chislehurst telephone code, IMP, but the town relinquishes reluctantly its honorary title, claimed in the days when a Napoleon conquered a corner of Kent two generations after another failed to do so.

Tragedy in the Thames

★

All through the second half of the 19th century, the Rosherville Gardens at Northfleet were a popular attraction for
Londoners, who came in their thousands by boat down the
river Thames to riverside resorts in Kent. One of the paddle
steamers they travelled on was the *Princess Alice*, one of a
number of large saloon steamers owned by the London
Steamboat Company, which ran daily excursions from London to Gravesend and Sheerness and back again.

On Tuesday, 3rd September 1878 – a bright, sunny late
summer day – the *Princess Alice* left London Bridge at
10.30 am with about 700 happy trippers on board.

Some of them left the boat at the Rosherville Pier, which
was the disembarkation point for Rosherville Gardens. From
there they flocked through the entrance into the 20 acres of
pleasure gardens west of Gravesend. There was a zoo and an
aviary, botanical gardens and a maze, tea rooms, bands
playing and all sorts of sideshows and stalls, including those
specialising in the famous Gravesend shrimps, which were
an attraction in themselves.

In the evening, there were illuminations, dances and balls
and two theatres, one enclosed which could seat a thousand
people and another open-air one.

Rosherville Gardens was a once-a-year day out for many
young Londoners, especially the children for whom it was a
very special treat indeed.

But, like all good things, a day out at Rosherville had to
come to an end. At 4.15 pm the *Princess Alice* left Sheerness

The paddle steamer Princess Alice.

and called at the Northfleet jetty at 6 pm. By the time it left there, it had about 800 people aboard, most of them women and children: happy, tired, mostly sorry the day was nearly over but quite glad to be heading home for bed, too.

On board a band was playing a tune called *Nancy Lee* and apart from a certain amount of inevitable high spirits, everyone was well-behaved and there was none of the drunkenness that would characterise the return trips of some of the later steamers.

The *Princess Alice* chugged serenely up river, past Beckton Gas Works and North Woolwich. Her captain, William Grinstead, stood on a paddle box, looking ahead into the gathering evening mist and giving orders to the crew, while at the helm was a man called John Eyres, a stand-in who had taken over at Gravesend from one of the regular crew members. He was an experienced river man although he had never taken the helm of such a large craft before.

Behind them, the sister-ship the *Duke of Teck* followed and behind her, the *Duke of Connaught* left Gravesend at 6.30. All carried homegoing Londoners from the day's revels in Kent.

The river trip under a clear sky, with just a light breeze and a hint of autumn mist to herald summer's ending,

110

The collier Bywell Castle *which ran down the* Princess Alice.

should have been the perfect ending to a splendid day out. In fact, though, for some 700 of the passengers and crew of the *Princess Alice* it was not just the end of the day, but the end of life itself.

At about 7.45 pm the steamer was in midstream, just off the City of London gas works at Beckton and just below North Woolwich Gardens in that stretch of the river known as Galleon's Reach.

Those on deck in the bows of the steamer saw the towering bulk of the collier *Bywell Castle* ahead. She was coming downstream under the command of Capt Thomas Harrison, but in the charge of pilot Christopher Dicks from Stepney, in ballast and heading for her home port of Newcastle.

As the two vessels approached each other, neither seemed sure what the other was doing. Later, Capt Harrison said his vessel was moving down river at half speed as they went through Galleons Reach and they were about at the centre of

111

the Reach when they saw the *Princess Alice* coming up Barking Reach.

He said: 'We ported our helm to keep over towards Trip-cock Point and as the two vessels neared each other we saw that the excursion steamer had ported and then, immediately afterwards, she showed her green (starboard) light close under our port bow.'

On the *Princess Alice*, Capt Grinstead could not make up his mind what the oncoming collier intended and he shouted: 'Where are you coming to?'

The steamer had slowed almost to a stop, waiting to see what course the *Bywell Castle* would take, but instead of taking avoiding action, she came straight for the paddle steamer, which took the impact of the other vessel's bows pretty well amidships on the port (left) side.

Down in the saloon, second steward William Law said afterwards that the first impact was not particularly heavy. He remarked to a stewardess that they must have bumped a barge alongside. But almost immediately there was a much greater impact and there could be no doubt then that there had been a serious collision.

Law ran and grabbed a young lady friend and took her out on to deck. Dragging her through the confusion to the rail, he hoisted her on to his shoulders and jumped overboard. He was a strong swimmer and he headed for the river bank. But the lady either slipped or was dragged off his shoulders and was lost.

He managed to grab hold of a man who was struggling in the water and held him up until they were both picked up by rescuers. During that time he could only watch while all around him hundreds of people drowned.

Passengers on the upper deck of the *Princess Alice* saw the collision coming. Most of them rushed aft as the collier's bows sliced through the paddle steamer, which began to sink at once. Some jumped and a few managed to clamber

Thames watermen were offered five shillings for every body recovered from the wrecked Princess Alice.

aboard the collier. Others tried to climb funnels and were badly burned before they fell back into the water and were drowned.

Some grabbed the *Bywell Castle*'s anchor chain and began to haul themselves up. They were hurled back to their deaths when, unaware, the collier dropped anchor.

The panic and pandemonium was frightful. The night air was filled with the shrieks of the drowning as hundreds of people jumped or were flung into the river.

As soon as those aboard the *Bywell Castle* realised what had happened, her whistle had sounded continuously to raise the alarm. Ropes were flung out all round her and anything that would float and keep people afloat was dropped into the water.

Dozens of small craft put out from both banks of the river within a very few minutes of the accident and there were sickening scenes as boatmen fought each other over bodies, for which they were being offered five shillings for every one recovered.

Some of the people struggling in the water, weighed down with heavy clothing made heavier with water, tried desperately to cling to the sides of the boats, threatening to overturn or sink them, so that they had to be beaten off and left to drown.

Within five minutes of the collision, the *Princess Alice* had sunk completely into about 18 feet of water. For a hundred yards, the river was full of drowning people screaming for help.

Only about 200 passengers and crew were saved. Some were picked up by a boat put out by the *Duke of Teck*. When the *Duke of Connaught* arrived on the scene it stayed on station for about half an hour while a boat was put out among the debris in the river to search for survivors, but none was found and the vessel carried on with its own unnaturally quiet complement of passengers and crew towards its London Bridge destination.

Some of the survivors and bodies were taken to the Royal Arsenal Pier, where the bodies were laid out in the boardroom of the company offices while the injured received attention at the town hall before being sent home. Others were taken to The Steam Packet public house at Woolwich and a temporary mortuary was opened in Woolwich town hall.

About 25 of the passengers were landed on the north side of the river, near the gas works. The rest were taken to the south (Kent) side. The *Princess Alice*'s captain, William Grinstead, and most of her crew, perished.

Dozens of heart-rending stories were told by survivors and rescuers afterwards. One young woman told how her baby was swept out of her arms and she lost her husband and three children. A man who jumped overboard with a lifebuoy round him told his wife to throw their children to him and then to jump herself. He lost them all.

The confusion was extreme and afterwards there were conflicting reports and accusations about what really happened.

Capt Harrison of the *Bywell Castle* said that immediately after the impact his crew threw out lifebuoys and lines and lowered boats to pick up bodies and survivors. Some of the survivors, however, were adamant that no lines were thrown from the collier for some moments, during which she seemed to be unaware of what had happened and continued on her way down river.

Legal representatives of both vessels each blamed the other for the collision, and for the catastrophic loss of life.

When the *Princess Alice* was lifted, divers found hundreds of bodies still on board, packed still upright in a gangway where the lower deck passengers had crowded as they fought to reach the upper deck.

The inquest went on until November and the jury could not agree a verdict until after they had been locked away all night. Then they returned a verdict – not unanimous, even then – that the collision was not wilful but that the *Bywell Castle* did not take the necessary precautions in time for easing, stopping and reversing her engines.

They decided the *Princess Alice* contributed to the collision by not stopping her engines and going astern. They also added that in their opinion such collisions might be avoided in future if proper and stringent rules were laid down for the navigation of all steam traffic in the river, and they added a rider that although the *Princess Alice* was seaworthy, she was not properly and efficiently manned and that she had a greater number of passengers on board than was prudent.

M. Blériot's Magnificent Success

★

There were only a few watchers on the cliffs of Dover that Sunday morning, 25th July 1909. Coastguards looked out across the Channel expectantly. Policemen on duty cast an eye in the general direction of the distant French coastline. A few journalists had gathered hopefully and a Frenchman, M Fontaine, peered seawards, an enormous French tricolour in his hands, ready to signal with it when the time came.

None of them knew just when that time would be. They did not even know for sure that Louis Blériot would be making his bid today to be the first to cross the Channel by aeroplane and to win the *Daily Mail* £1,000 prize for doing so.

In fact, though, M. Blériot had been up and about on the French side of the Channel since 2.30 that morning. He had been waiting several days for the right weather conditions. On Saturday afternoon, a westerly wind had been blowing at 40–50 mph until about 7 pm, but by 8.30 it had dropped very considerably and the aeronaut went to bed at the Terminus Hotel in Calais hopeful that conditions would be as near perfect as he could hope for by dawn the next morning.

He left the hotel at 3 am with his friend M. Le Blanc and went by motor car to Baraques, near Sangatte. He had an injured leg and was still using crutches and sticks to walk with. That morning, the leg was very painful and, had the stakes been less high, or the man less determined, the flight might even then have been called off.

The aeroplane, the *Blériot XI* (so-called because it was M. Blériot's eleventh aircraft), was waiting in a temporary garage at Baraques. While the front of the shelter was raised in readiness for the machine to be trundled out, instructions were sent to the destroyer *Escopette* to be ready to sail.

The destroyer had been put at the disposal of the venture by the French government, to escort the little aircraft and both to make sure the flight was completed in accordance with the rules of the competition and to be ready to rescue the flier if that became necessary.

Garden railings round the shelter were taken up and, with the help of a volunteer ground crew, the little plane was wheeled out through a narrow opening between two houses on to a flat grassy area between the old castle at Calais and the sand dunes of the French coastline.

M. Blériot limped along behind it until it was out in the open. While the plane was held down by five men, he was helped up into the cockpit, where he settled himself for the great adventure.

It was 4.10 in the morning by the time all the necessary checks and preparations were completed. A short test flight of about ten miles was made and then, by 4.30, it was judged to be sufficiently light to satisfy the competition condition that the crossing must take place in daylight.

A light breeze was blowing from the south-west and Blériot was dressed in blue cotton overalls over a khaki wool-lined jacket, which he wore on top of his tweed suit. A close fitting cap covered his head and ears.

Louis Blériot was no novice at flying aeroplanes. He was already veteran of a number of long-distance flights and he was well aware of how cold it could be up there in the empty spaces of the sky.

The Daily Mail, which put up the prize, also carried the full story of the historic flight of Louis Bleriot.

118

At 4.41 French time, the plane finally took off to make the first powered flight across the Channel.

The pilot had to give his machine almost maximum speed as he headed towards Sangatte in order to clear the coastal telegraph wires. Then, safely airborne, he turned right and crossed the French coast at 4.42.

The *Escopette* was already at sea, but was caught just a little unprepared. It had to re-set its course to keep the little monoplane in sight and while it did so, the plane outdistanced it.

Flying at a height of about 250 ft above the sea at a speed of something over 40 mph and with no compass to guide him, Blériot set his course by the direction in which the destroyer was travelling. But since the ship had a maximum speed of only about 26 knots, he soon left it behind.

He estimated he reached something approaching 60 mph during part of the journey.

As he himself said afterwards: 'At one point I looked around and saw nothing. For ten minutes I was lost and just let the plane take its own course.'

He experienced an eerie few minutes over a featureless sea in a featureless sky. All his previous flights had been over land and he had always been able to navigate by roads and railways and other easily recognisable landmarks. Now there was nothing.

But the engine was running perfectly, the aircraft was perfectly under control, the wind was just right; even though he had no way of knowing if he was steering a true course or not, he was not unduly worried.

Then, 20 minutes after leaving France, he saw the white cliffs of Dover and the castle on top of them.

The wind, which was much stronger now than when he had taken off, was taking him off course towards St Margaret's Bay and the Goodwin Sands, so he turned west, intending to land on open grassland behind the castle.

He was first spotted by the watchers on the cliff tops just before 5 am. At that time he was heading for St Margaret's Bay, passing over ships of the Atlantic Fleet lying at anchor inside the Dover breakwater. He steered straight for them and passed between two of the vessels as he made for the coast.

Blériot's friend Fontaine, the man with the French flag, was waiting for him. When he spotted the little aircraft approaching the English coast, he unfurled the flag and began to wave it vigorously to attract the pilot's attention and direct him to a suitable landing place. Blériot waved back to acknowledge the signal and then prepared to land.

He said afterwards it was the most difficult landing he had ever performed. Caught by an eddying wind between the castle and the opposite hill, he was whirled round several times. In the end, he simply stopped the engine and let the plane fall some 65 feet to the ground on to Northfall Meadows. Contemporary reports described it as 'a perfect landing'!

At once, a group of khaki-clad soldiers and a uniformed policeman ran towards him, closely followed by two Frenchmen who had been waiting for this moment for days.

Blériot was helped out of the cockpit, handed his crutches, which he accepted with some relief, for his leg was painful again after his struggle with the foot-controlled rudder bar in the fresh wind over Dover, and was escorted triumphantly to the nearby Lord Warden Hotel.

Most of the people of Dover missed the historic arrival above their town. The cross-Channel flight had taken so little time that signals which had been intended to alert them to the Frenchman's coming had remained unused.

Nevertheless, it was not long before word spread and a crowd of excited onlookers gathered around the flimsy-looking little craft, 23 feet long and made of ash and poplar

The cover of the souvenir programme of the Luncheon given by the Daily Mail to honour Louis Blériot's cross-channel flight.

wood stiffened with piano strings so that it weighed only 45 pounds.

Asked if he would make the crossing again, Blériot said he had no doubt at all that he could do so, but thought he would not because he had promised his wife that, after a race for which he was already entered, he would fly no more.

Back on the French coast, journalists and others gathered at the Channel tunnel workings at Sangatte to be first to hear of the successful landing in England by wireless telegraph there. The news came through at six o'clock that morning. Blériot had arrived safely in a meadow near Dover Castle. The prize was his.

Blériot himself declared that, happy as he was to have won the £1,000, it was more important to be the first to cross the Channel by aeroplane than to have won the prize.

News of the feat went around the world. One journalist, seeking an 'angle' on the story, woke up the American pioneer aviator Wilbur Wright and asked for his comments on the Channel flight.

Mr Wright made the slightly barbed comment that the news compensated for his broken slumbers, but he thought his brother's projected flight over hill and dale and woodland between Fort Myer and Alexandria would surpass the Frenchman's because the air pressures would be vastly greater.

Blériot received the *Daily Mail* prize at a celebrity luncheon in London on Monday, 21st July. He travelled from Dover with his wife in a special saloon carriage attached to the regular service train and was mobbed when he arrived at Victoria, by a huge crowd of sightseers.

His little plane was brought to London where it was exhibited to a sensation-hungry public, free of charge, in the motor accessories and sports department of Selfridge's Oxford Street store – a promotional coup for which Selfridge's contributed £200 to charity.

The flight was reported in the *Kent Messenger* on 31st July, under the headline: M. Blériot's Magnificent Success.

According to that report, the somewhat zig-zag flight covered about 31 miles in about 43 minutes – 'a flight so rapid that the attendant torpedo boat was left hopelessly behind.'

The paper expressed sympathy for Mr Herbert Latham, an Englishman who had been Blériot's closest rival for the cash and the glory of being the first man to fly an aeroplane across the Channel.

He nearly did it. On his first attempt his machine flew about one-third of the way before it developed a fault and had to be brought down in the sea, where it floated until the flyer could be rescued.

Less than a week before the Blériot success, Latham had set off from Sangatte and was within two miles of Dover's Admiralty Pier head when he again had to 'ditch'. That time, his nose was broken and he received other injuries.

He did not even have the solace of knowing his flight was largely unobserved, as Blériot would have done if the same fate had befallen him. Thousands of people along the English coast had been waiting to cheer their countryman to victory and, instead, witnessed his humiliation. Nevertheless, they cheered him enthusiastically when he was brought ashore by steam pinnace and taken to the Lord Warden Hotel.

Latham was all ready to make another attempt when Blériot beat him to it. Like Blériot, he had gone to bed the night before aware that wind conditions were improving and, in order to get a good night's sleep, he gave his alarm clock into the safe keeping of one of his team with orders to wake him if the weather promised to be suitable.

Unfortunately, his friends were over-anxious for his safety and misread the weather signs. They left it too late before they roused him for the attempt.

By the time Latham was ready, M. Blériot had already soared off into the pages of aviation history, leaving the unhappy Mr Latham to be one of the first to send his warmest congratulations to the first man to cross the English Channel in an aeroplane.

Index